BEAR IT ALL

2011-2012

Edited by
Alex Portera, Sean Fischer, Sam Werboff and
Cody Kittle

Kiva
Loans that Change Lives

Bear It All is proud to announce that
100% of profits from sales
are put to use in fighting global poverty.

The money is lent to entrepreneurs through Kiva, a microfinance website that helps alleviate poverty by connecting individual lenders with business owners in developing countries.

Entrepreneurs sometime seek out loans for as little as $100 to get small businesses going.

The first edition of *Bear It All* issued more than 50 loans to people in Kyrgyzstan, Bolivia, Tanzania, Nicaragua, The Democratic Republic of the Congo, Armenia, Iraq, Mongolia, Togo, and many other countries around the world.

It's a large impact for a reader like you to have. We thank you for joining Bear It All's mission to create value and end global poverty.

Check it all out at:
www.kiva.org/lender/BearItAll

Tene Morou
Togo
Clothing

Gayane
Armenia
Agriculture

A few of the 50+ entrepreneurs *Bear It All* has supported

Masinavaaia Apulu
Samoa
Baking

Mrs. Sangha Nheanh
Cambodia
Pig Breeding

Jaques
Rwanda
Food Production

Lureen
Palestine
Grocery Stores

Bear It All Disclaimer

Bear It All is an **UNOFFICIAL** publication that is neither affiliated with nor endorsed by Washington University in St. Louis. The opinions expressed in this publication are not those of Washington University.

Bear It All is intended to be an unofficial Wash. U. student companion, written in a manner that is casual and humorous. It has no affiliation with the faculty, staff, or administration of Washington University. **Bear It All** is intended to be an unofficial advice book, written with a candor that other University publications cannot match because of their associations, responsibilities, and liabilities.

For all OFFICIAL information, see Washington University's website at www.wustl.edu, or contact the proper University representative. Wash. U.'s OFFICIAL Student Guide Handbook is an excellent and easily accessible wealth of information. That publication is the recognized handbook for students at Washington University. Our book, **Bear It All**, is in no way designed to compete with or to replace Wash. U.'s Student Guide. For the final say on all official matters, consult with Wash. U.'s Student Guide.

The writers, editors, designers, and illustrators of this book would like to say that we are in NO WAY responsible or liable for bad ideas or actions that anyone might take because of **Bear It All**. Many things that students do at college are outrageous and imbecilic. Although we document and describe many traditions at Wash. U., we do not recommend anything that will endanger you or anyone else. This book is written to help students et. al. enjoy their time at Wash. U. while sacrificing neither life nor limb.

Some rules that need to be established now are rules that you should already know. First, don't do anything illegal! Don't drink underage, don't drink and drive, don't use illegal drugs, don't steal, or vandalize property! If you choose to do something illegal, it is your own responsibility to deal with the consequences.

Next, don't do anything that is going to hurt you or your friends. Use alcohol responsibly. If you or your friends are ever in trouble, suck it up and tell someone in an authority position IMMEDIATELY. It will always be worth it.

Moreover, obey University rules! If you do not, you may fail classes, be thrown out of housing, be expelled from the University, or arrested.

Lastly, be accountable for yourself. Make the decisions that you know are right and you'll always be fine. So if you think you have an idea of how to act or what to do because of this book, and this idea is illegal,

Bear It All Disclaimer

dangerous, against University policies, or just downright stupid, then DON'T DO IT! If you do attempt something stupid, don't say we didn't warn you! We wrote and published **Bear It All** to make life for students easier, happier, and healthier. So please don't do anything to make your life, or the life of others, anything contrary to our goals.

The writers, editors, designers and illustrators of **Bear It All** would like to say that what we have written is in no way fact, nor do we claim it to be; we have written this book to provide well intentioned advice, entertainment, and humor. Any and all information within is subject to change. The things we have documented represent our feelings toward life at Wash. U. We have done our best to be even-handed and objective, but because of our proximity to this school (all people involved are, or were, Wash. U. students) we necessarily suffer under a prejudice of subjectivity. The feelings and opinions expressed in **Bear It All**, like any, are fallible. However, in instances when we are not being humorous or satirical, we have done our very best to report the truth. We have in no way intentionally or maliciously reported falsehoods about an individual or institution; we have in no way attempted to slander an individual or institution; and we have set out only to report our opinions and to in no way falsely indict an individual's or institution's character or integrity.

If you or any party that you represent feel mistreated by this book, know that what lies within represents only the opinions of the writers, editors, designers and illustrators of Bear It All. In many instances, not all of the parties involved agree with the opinions espoused in **Bear It All**! Furthermore, the charities mentioned in this publication that the editors of **Bear It All** have chosen to donate money to are in NO WAY affiliated with this publication.

We have expressed these opinions for the reasons stated above, and we do so with our right to free speech kept carefully in mind. Lastly, if we have misrepresented you or your interests, please contact us so that we might rectify such mistakes in subsequent publications.

All contents within this edition of **Bear It All** are the intellectual property of Alex Portera, Sean Fischer, Sam Werboff, and Cody Kittle. The content of this book may not be copied or reproduced in any form whatsoever, without the expressed written consent of Alex Portera, Sean Fischer, Sam Werboff or Cody Kittle.

Enjoy our book, be safe, and have a great time while at Wash. U.!

Dedication

If the day you opened that letter was one of the happiest days of your life,

If you applied early or turned down the Ivys,

If Wash. U. is your friends, family, and home,

If you are proud to add the "In St. Louis",

Then this book is dedicated to you.

Acknowledgements

We would like to take this page to thank everyone who contributed to help make **Bear It All** happen. Through the good times and the bad, people have stuck with us and made this book possible. With over 70 people contributing to this book, we can truly say it is a guide by students for students. For all those who contributed, we thank you.

We'd like to thank Sherveen Mashayekhi for his work as our Director of Sales and Marketing.

We'd like to thank Cody Kittle for his support, his ideas, and doing the things we couldn't figure out how to do.

We'd like to thank Zoë Scharf for the amazing work she did designing the cover art.

Table of Contents

Table of Contents

Themes in *Bear It All*

This book is a collaboration. We have reached out to students, faculty, and alumni from all over Wash. U. to contribute to this book. Our hope was that by having a diverse base of writers, the book would end up providing an unbiased look at Wash. U. Unfortunately this is impossible, and there is plenty of bias in this book. Sean, Sam, and I are all 2011 grads who hung out in the same group of friends and enjoyed similar things. We tried to dilute this by getting others to heavily contribute to the book. But all students have their own histories, interests, and biases towards the school. What you get when you combine articles from such a diverse base of writers is not a solid objective book, but an amorphous blob of ideas and opinions about what Wash. U. is and should be like. We tried to make this book as factual and informative as possible, but at times we inevitably slipped from this model.

To this end, we would like to open with a few of the themes that you will notice throughout the book. If you are aware of these themes, it will help you better understand the book, and help you filter out the things you need to know from the things that you don't.

1. *The more information, the better.* We built this book to provide as much information about Wash. U. as possible. Because we have no professional ties to the school, we are able to provide information the school cannot. Ultimately we think this is a good thing.

2. *Wash. U. students are not that attractive.* But you didn't need our book to know that.

3. *Learning is important, but so is being social.* You are at one of the best Universities in the world. You are here to learn as much as possible and set yourself up for a life of success, excitement, and fulfillment. Some of this will come from class, but a lot will come from what you do outside of class. Learning how to be social, to interact with others and get along with people who are different from you is just as important as what

you learn in the classroom. Students at Wash. U. are notorious for their intense study habits, which is great, but we hope that you can learn to have a little more fun while you're at it (not that orgo isn't a rager).

4. *You were smart enough to get into this school, so you are smart enough to use this information wisely.* When we talk about drinking, smoking, or doing other potentially dangerous things, we do so with the belief that you are responsible for your own actions. You should never put yourself in a compromising situation, and you should always use your best judgment when making decisions. You should not make important decisions solely based on the information in our book.

Letter from the Editor
Reflection

By Alex Portera

What is **Bear It All**? Why did Sean, Sam, and I make it? Who is it for? Who are we?

What is Bear it All?

    Bear It All is the unofficial underground guide to all things Wash. U. With contributions from over 70 students, perhaps the best part about this book is the simple fact that it is written by experienced students for incoming students. These are kids that have been there before, seen and done the best and the worst, and are ready to give you the inside scoop on on greek life, social life, academic life, and everything in between.

Why did we make Bear It All?

    When contemplating the potential of **Bear It All**, we discussed the pros and cons of publishing an underground university guide. In the end we realized that the insights into Wash. U. that we could provide through our own experiences, and the experiences of over 70 other students would be an invaluable tool for anyone interested in Wash. U. outside of its ranking.

    I can remember clear as day the anxieties and worries, in addition to my excitement and anticipation before the first day of class. Would I make friends? Would I like being so far from home? Would I be able to get any good Italian food (not really)? **Bear It All** is not going to remove these anxieties; they are a natural part of the transition into college. However, **Bear It All** will provide readers with a comprehensive, although biased, view of Wash. U. life.

    While lugging your bags up the stairs of your freshman dorm, the hot and humid St. Louis air will prove to be a great icebreaker for conversation with your fellow floormates. As you learn about each other things will settle down, and in a few weeks you will be acclimated to Wash. U. That doesn't mean you will know everything. Any upperclassman can attest to this fact. Sean, Sam and I hope that Bear It All will help you prove them wrong.

Who is this book for?

While **Bear It All** will be most useful for freshman, it is also written for nervous parents, potential applican'ts (with nervous parents), alumni looking to catch up with the current state of affairs at their alma matter, current students curious about what such a book could be about, and anyone who wants to know more about the school we call Washington University in St. Louis. Even if you think you know it all, we dare you to read on, you may learn a thing or two.

Who are we?

Three guys who want to make this world a better place any way we can...especially when it involves imparting knowledge on the young future of this great University.

With all that said, we sincerely hope you enjoy our 2011-2012 edition of **Bear It All**.

Alex Portera
Executive Editor, Class of 2011

Sean Fischer
Executive Editor, Class of 2011

Sam Werboff
Executive Editor, Class of 2011

I

History, etc.

"To those of you who received honors,
awards and distinctions, I say well done.
And to the C students, I say you too may one
day be president of the United States."

George W. Bush

History of Wash. U.

With all the information there is to offer concerning Washington University in St. Louis, where do we begin? Well, from the beginning...

In 1853, there were two men—Wayman Crow and William Greenleaf Eliot—who led the effort in establishing a place for higher education in the Midwest. Crow was a state senator at the time, and Eliot, a Unitarian minister, was the grandfather of Nobel Prize laureate poet T. S. Eliot. Despite Eliot's attempt to raise money through solicitations, he failed to secure any kind of permanent endowment for the school. Wash. U. tried to get on its feet with no religious backing, no money, and no governmental support.

The school's name has changed multiple times throughout its establishment. In its beginnings Wash. U. went by the name of Eliot Seminary. However, Wash. U. has never been a religious university, and in 1854 the name was changed to Washington Institute—after George Washington. The decision to use Washington's name was timely. The American Civil War was on the horizon, and Washington was a symbol of national unity during a period of national division. In 1856, the name was changed once again to Washington University, and in 1976 "in St. Louis" was added to avoid the common confusion with the fine university in Seattle.

Since its founding, Wash. U. has taken tremendous strides to increase its impact on the world. In 1904, Wash. U. hosted the World's fair, where the invention of the waffle-cone was first presented. Holmes lounge was actually built for the fair, as a place to present the Queen of England's jewels. Professor Compton conducted a series of experiments to prove the particle nature of electromagnetic radiation, earning him a Nobel Prize for the "Compton effect" in 1927. In 1947, Professor Corti at the School of Medicine discovered the biochemical pathway for glycogen degredation, a cycle that became known as the "Cori cycle" and earned the school its fifth and sixth Nobel laureates (if you couldn't tell, the school has some strong foundations in the sciences). By 1957, the school began planning the construction of the "South 40" (on-campus housing that would raise awareness about the University to the nation as a whole as opposed to only appealing to locals who could commute from home daily). In 1992, 2000, and 2004 Wash. U. played host to the presidential debates, and was most recently the site of the vice presidential debates between Sarah Palin and Joe Biden.

Today, Wash. U. has grown to be the 13th best school in the nation according to US News & World Report. The different schools within the University have also kept pace with the overarching rising prestige. You have chosen well, and you are in good hands. The resources and support you need to be as successful as you want are here for you. Now make Crow and Eliot proud by learning a thing or two.

Wash. U.phamisms

1) Hard CLASS - cl., The kids who get A's are the kids who could have gone to an Ivy, but chose Wash. U. instead. See any pre-med, architecture, BME (biomedical engineering) or 400-level philosophy course.

2) Easy CLASS - cl., The kids who don't get A's missed class because they were too hungover. See UCollege courses, music lessons, and lower-level psychology courses.

Throughout the book you will find numerous Wash. U.phamisms, the lingo of Wash. U. 's campus. Use this key for help indentifying the part of speech: pl.- place e.- event cl.-campus lingo

17

Mascot

While Wash. U.'s mascot may raise the school spirit of parents more than its students, there is an interesting history behind our beloved Bear. In the early 1900's we were called the Pikers, named after The Pike, an amusement section at the 1904 World's Fair of the same name that spanned across Lindell between Skinker and Debaliviere. On December 18, 1925 students voted to change the mascot to the bear. Originally this mascot manifested itself in a live black bear cub that was donated to the University. In the late 1930's a logo of an angry looking bear with a sailor cap was created, named the Battling Bear. No one knows exactly why the bear had a sailor cap, but he was an irrefutable badass. In 1994, the Battling Bear was replaced by a new bear drawn by a Wash. U. student that is a bit more, well, bearlike. Nevertheless, we proudly declare that we are the Wash. U. Bears to anyone who steps on our turf, especially when NYU comes to town. The Voilets, what a joke. Our other unofficial mascot is the Thinker on the Rock, or more lovingly, the Anorexic Bunny. Located in the middle of campus between the Olin Library and Mallinkrodt sits our creepy, ponderous bunny. The bunny is associated with various student groups, and is one of the most recognizable landmarks at Wash. U.

School Colors

In the 1890's, Wash. U. chose to make our school colors Red and Green. Officially the colors are "a rich red and green," even if they do look like Christmas colors.

Logo

In the 1980's the school created a committee tasked to design a more recognizable logotype, which is now seen all over campus and on the bumper stickers of proud parents. The logotype involves a shield, two bars, and three stars, which are from the coat of arms of George Washington. We can also see a fleur-de-lis, the symbol of St. Louis and the French King Louis IX, and the name of our university.

History

II

Wash. U.
Academics

"I was thrown out of college for cheating on the metaphysics exam: I looked into the soul of another boy."

Woody Allen

Art Sci

Spanning over 20 departments and even more disciplines in thereof, the College of Arts and Sciences is by far the biggest school within Washington University. Arts and Sciences houses the most undergraduates of any college and claims many of the infamous pre-med students. Unlike art or architecture students who tend to live in claustrophobic studios, Art Sci students typically congregate in the Olin library. While study times for Art Sci students vary greatly depending on major, its been said that the pre-meds become so acclimated to life inside Olin that the outdoor air becomes unpalatable, likely due to curricularly-induced hypochondriasis. Have no fear though, Art Sci has an incredibly wide range of majors, from education to economics, so you'll have no problem finding your niche. Albeit, whatever that niche is, it's likely that you'll be joining the pre-meds in the library for a fair portion of your time.

The Art Sci college is where you'll find all the bio students, along with the linguist majors and the poli sci fanatics. Its most distinguishable by the fact that the students in this school are not set on a particular kind of professional track. While those in the Sam Fox may only have an idea of the type of job they desire, they typically know that they want design and visual arts to be a part of their daily lives. While some Art Sci students find their passion in a particular discipline and pursue it early on, others may choose to dabble in a variety of areas and experience a true liberal arts perspective. The takeaway here is that Art Sci is what you make of it. You can mold your education in fantastic ways to best suit you're own college needs. In Art Sci, more than any other school, you will find students who are unsure of what the future brings, and in the opinion of many: surely this is not a bad thing.

Along with any upside of Art Sci is that ever present downside, and that downside is that besides preparing you for graduate school, most majors do not have any direct real-world application. The Avenue Q song *What Do You Do With A B.A. in English?* definitely has some truth to it. You will have learned invaluable critical thinking, writing, communication etc. skills, but those skills are hard to fully display in a thirty minute interview. And yet, there is light at the end of the tunnel. Many jobs are not major specific, and most employers

Academics

understand that the skills you earn as a liberal arts major will make you successful in the workplace. You just might need to put in a little extra effort to explain to an interviewer why the philosophy major should get the I-Banking job over the finance major.

To close with one last bit of advice—don't commit to a major too early. It's great if you know what you want, but there is something beautiful about shopping around for a major. You have until sophomore year to commit, and to pursue something because you think it's what you love is different than pursuing something because you love it. Enjoy the College of Arts and Sciences, to its fullest potential.

Wash. U.phamisms

3) Rager - e., A party atypical of the Wash. U. social scene. This party likely had a keg and hard liquor, as well as more than 15 people. It was probably also off-campus, and broken up by the police for a noise complaint around 11:30. But man was it sick - they had a kegorator and Beatles Rockband!
4) Linus - e., Some would say Linus is the best social event of the year. A 21+ event, Linus is a formal attire, student-run fundraiser with a live band and open bar. Everyone who is anyone attends, and is surely looking their best.

Art School

You don't need to sleep, and in any case you can't afford it. You need x-acto knives by the dozen, spray fixative, and several hundred fonts to get you started. You need to be ready to put in long hours pursuing purposefully vague suggestions. You need to be "creative" on deadline. You need coffee. You need somebody to drive you to the obscure store 45 minutes into Illinois to buy 16-inch non-coated copper wire or off-white recycled cardstock. You need to stop scratching the paper so loudly when you doodle in business classes. You need lots of micron pens. You need to remember not to wear sandals on days that you are going to use power tools. You need coffee. You don't need sleep.

The art school is different, for sure. For such a seemingly loose field it's surprising to see that your time becomes more structured than your pre-med roommate. I'm not saying it's harder, just unrelenting. There is no time when there is nothing to worry about until a midterm in two weeks. You hang your homework on the wall every day for your class and professors to look at, which means that if you spent the night playing drunken Mario Kart, everybody knows. For many this is better than a setup that allows for weeks of procrastination, because they would take full advantage, but it gets a bit grueling.

This sounds negative. If this was the way accounting or investment banking were taught it's almost guaranteed that there would be a lot fewer takers. The redeeming factor is that you are getting to do what you love which does, actually, somehow make it blissfully okay. Most assignments have the potential to become something you are really proud of--or to be discarded immediately, on less inspiring occasions. The point is that the work means something to you. Not necessarily in an "I'm doing a painting about my feelings" sort of way but at least in the sense that you get to work to be as good as you can at something that you have likely cared about for a long time. When you hang up your work at 4:00am and come back for critique four hours later to find it looking better than you had realized, it's kind of special. Then you get back to it, fuck sleep.

Engineering

If you spent your childhood building Lego's or taking things apart just to see how they worked, the engineering school at Wash. U. might be for you. Be warned. Engineering, especially at schools like Wash. U., is hard. If you decide to go into the engineering school, you will find yourself immersed in more math and science than you know what to do with. If you like these subjects you'll do very well, and if you don't you're in for a surprise. Many people get into engineering thinking that they will spend their days building hover cars and testing out jet-packs, but real engineering is simply the practical application of applied science. The engineering school at Wash. U. tends to teach more theory-based engineering, with only a few classes where you have labs in order to experiment and learn more about the real world application of some topics. If you like physics, engineering should be a strong contender in the battle to choose your major.

One of the first things you'll notice when you begin your career in the engineering school is how incredibly smart your professors are. After admiring this brilliance, you will soon notice how it can, at times, prohibit their ability to teach undergraduates. The Engineering school does have many outstanding teaching professors, but Wash. U. hires faculty based on their ability to do research for the school. There are both pros and cons to this situation. Though you get professors that are experts in their field and extremely good at what they do, many of these professors have a Ph.D. in the field that they teach and don't realize that what seems simple to them is completely foreign to undergraduate students.

Besides this fact, the engineering school as a whole is extremely supportive. Unlike many cutthroat engineering schools of the same caliber, you will find that most of your peers are happy to help you with anything you are having trouble with, and almost every professor will be available to answer questions. You will have classes where you feel like you have no idea what is going on. Don't assume that you'll get it later - ask questions! (Politely) pester the professor until you understand exactly what is going on. It may seem like you're being annoying, but they want you to learn the material. And it is almost certain that if you have a question, someone else in the room has the same one. Professors are glad to help you if you feel you are in over your head, but you need to reach out to them first.

25

The best piece advice to give if you decide to join the engineering school (and any other school for that matter), is to stay organized and on top of what you need to be doing. Start assignments early. You don't need to finish them right away, but the earlier you start, the better prepared you will be to understand what is expected out you.

If you're someone that likes math and science and enjoys working hard to learn a topic that is extremely useful and rewarding, the engineering school is something you should seriously consider. While it is a lot of work, everyone that sticks with it loves engineering by the end, and can't imagine having pursued anything else.

Architecture

Architecture students at Wash. U. are most certainly known for their elusive nature and mysterious ways. They will be gone for many hours and sometimes even days as they claim to be at this place called "studio" somewhere past the arches of Brookings. Where exactly they are and what exactly they all could be doing for so many hours on any given night of the week remains a mystery to most students. The situation becomes even more confusing when the next time you see them they have bags under their eyes and it looks like they haven't slept in days. With signs like these, some have come to the belief that this Given Hall is actually Club Givens and the architecture majors are simply up all night partying. What could they possibly be working on for so long anyway? Contrary to this appealing rumor, architecture students do have the heaviest workload for any major (yes even more than BME). The reason comes from the combination of the high demands from the professors and the fact that most architecture students are very passionate and meticulous about their work.

Architecture models and drawings are not exactly like your average test or paper that can be rushed at the last minute without much care. Architects spend a lot of time and effort redoing and reworking their projects as the workload increases every year. One common misconception about the work is that it simply involves drawing floor plans and making cute models of homes straight from freshmen year. However, architecture projects start off very conceptual: focusing more on abstract patterns and learning how to draw. As time goes on architecture projects focus more and more on the design and structure of actual spaces and buildings. With the heavy workload, the amount of time spent together in studio, and the required classes that go along with an architecture major, the students definitely form a strong camaraderie with one another and a work hard play hard(er) mentality to go along with it. Despite the work, it's not so surprising to see many architects out on Friday night partying it up--even with the minimal sleep they may have gotten in nights prior. As with any difficult courseload at Wash. U., architecture will not be easy. That being said, if you have the passion, this program will give you a solid foundation for building your future.

Academics

Business

"B-School pre-school" is the virtually ubiquitous refrain of students from other disciplines at Wash. U. They claim that their derision comes from the fact that B-school coursework is easy and light, and the four day school week attracts party-loving trust-funders looking for an easy ride. Blunt B-schoolers will tell you that their fellow students are just jealous of the fat paychecks and three-letter job titles starting with a C that await them after graduation. There may be some truth to both of these claims, but Olin is the undisputed home of entrepreneurial, career-savvy, and upwardly mobile students at Wash. U.

In an effort to cultivate the next generation of managers, the Olin administration has put a heavy emphasis on group work and presentations. Whether you're making strategic recommendations on Southwest Airlines, or analyzing Soviet negotiation tactics during the Cuban Missile Crisis, presenting will be an integral part of your time in the B-school. Buy yourself a suit - you'll need it. If presenting isn't exactly your thing and you're shooting to be the next hot-shot trader at Goldman, try going the Finance route. You'll enjoy a little more number crunching, but may have to suffer through self-important assholes that raise their hands during class and try to subtly mention their portfolio returns.

No matter what B-school major you choose to pursue, you get to enjoy the benefits of the Weston Career Center—a staff of trained advisers who are there to help you land that dream internship or full-time position. The professors are also remarkably connected, and you'll find more than a handful who have left lucrative private-sector positions to come teach at Olin. The B-school sports multiple presentation rooms, an exclusive computer lab, lounge areas, and a Bloomberg terminal if you have an itching to pull a Madoff. Einstein Bagels, the most recent addition to Simon hall, continues to be a popular destination for both B-schoolers and the general masses.

The students of the B-school do know how to have a good time, but they are unequivocally focused on their careers. For jobs at top firms, this means having an uber-high GPA and stellar internships throughout your college career. With all the talk of how easy the B-school is, if you want to come out successful, you need to be prepared to work hard. If you make it, I hear they wrap keys to an M-Series in your diploma.

Understanding the B-School Group Meeting

A very important facet of getting good grades in the B-School is conquering the group meeting. B-School assignments are generally case-oriented and rely on group collaboration. There are a lot of nuances to being productive in a group setting, especially when that group often includes friends, foes, and flirts.

Groups are either selected randomly by the professor or by the students themselves. In the random groups you will usually encounter a few specific types of people time and time again. The people that succeed are actually the ones who put in the most effort, while the lazy stoner (LS) in the group will most likely suffer. Because the group assignments culminate with a peer performance evaluation, people are vigilant of free riding (letting your group do the all of the work), and will put in the effort to make sure their grade and reputation do not suffer. An honest effort, even from Cheech or Chong, can still earn a neutral performance evaluation. The bane of the LS's laid back attitude is the alpha: a know-it-all, overly serious individual who thinks his or her shit doesn't stink and will force the LS into submission, MMA style. Though the alpha will keep the group on top of their work, reason is not an option for these people and despite their motivations they can sometimes be counterproductive to the group environment. The secretary will also emerge, who will flood your inbox to probe for the next meeting on an assignment due in a month. While annoying at first, this is an invaluable service, because you may not have the foresight to plan a day in advance, nevermind a month. Then there are the worker bees. These people sit quietly and do the work they are assigned to do, usually in an acceptable manner, but do not stir the pot. In the end, random group's projects are much more thorough, maximize total contribution, most conducive to learning the class's intended principles, and might even help you make a few new friends.

Self-selected groups are much more relaxed. The aforementioned characters still appear but are grouped far more homogeneously. This means that power groups emerge and treat the subject matter as if it were the next presidential election. The frat groups will also surface, doing their best Animal House impressions for each other. However, it is the "Revenge of the Nerds" group that usually gets the best grades (if you've seen the movie you know they always win). However, for the more typical group, repetitive meetings of recapping previous week's social events and deciding what to do the next weekend often come at the expense of getting the assignment done. These groups rely more

Academics

heavily on the delegation of assignments and utilize more concerted editing and revising efforts so that the final piece, if not revolutionary, is at the least coherent. These groups often vary based on the types of friends you have, so it is difficult to generalize, but the fact that you have personal relationships with these people can stand in the way of a polished product. Free riding is at its peak in these groups, though peer evaluations are no longer a real worry. These groups can be more entertaining, and might help you succeed with a someone you've been eyeing at the next frat party, but as the hours go by and nothing is done you'll feel the pain, which sucks when you have a test the next day and don't even know what QBA stands for.

3 Majors You Know

Biology

There definitely isn't a shortage of biology majors here at Wash. U. To many students, it's a simple way to fulfill all the med school prerequisites and obtain a major at the same time. Others seek one of the top biology departments in the country. Although it's not necessary for students to choose a particular field, the biology department allows individuals to follow tracks in neuroscience, molecular biology, genetics, evolution, etc.

As a bio major, you can expect to start out in huge introductory science classes with 200 or more students. Usually, all of these have three exams plus a cumulative final. The amount of material you cover for each exam is substantial but not impossible. If you ever have a hard time trying to find a spot to study in Olin library, chances are the bio students already took the good ones. A nice perk is that the intro classes are all taped and are available online as to stream in case you miss class (or just never go). Some people definitely just watch the videos instead of classes and some ending up doing okay. Others don't, but to each his own.

The Wash. U. biology department provides a very wide variety of classes. After the intro courses, students can try more specific ones like Principles of the Nervous System, Evolution and Microbiology. These classes are challenging and informative for those interested in science. One class that deserves mention is Physiological Control Systems (Bio 3058). You'll hear many things about this class, good and bad. Honestly, it's definitely worth taking to improve your testing skills (crucial for the MCAT), but at the same time it requires an obnoxious amount of work for a 2-credit course.

If biology is your choice of study here at Wash. U., be ready for a lot of studying. And yet the hard work pays off as Wash. U.'s bio courses are some of the best in the world to provide you with knowledge useful for careers in medicine, health or research. Just be ready to break the relationship you had with sleep for a new love: coffee.

Psychology

It will seem like almost every person on your freshman floor is taking Psych 100- the dry, all-encompassing introductory course every campus advisor recommends. Students who end up in this standard lecture will find themselves in one of two positions: They hate the material (especially the rigid multiple-choice tests) and decide to end their psychology coursework right there or they happily decide to go on and become psychology majors. That's about it.

A psychology major here at Wash. U. has a pretty easy existence. The major requirements are minimal and easy to complete, even if you decide to head down this path late in the game. Courses generally follow the same standard lecture format (of varying sizes, if you prefer more discussion-based courses you can definitely find some here) with between 3-5 tests over the course of the semester. For almost all of these classes you can certainly get away with doing negligible work until a few days before an exam, and then spending those days leading up to it cramming, though a lot of the material is actually very interesting and worth spending your time with. You will also find that many of the professors themselves have participated in the research discussed in the texts and are prominent in their respective fields.

One thing you will quickly find out is that many of the courses require students to participate in lab experiments through the department. Usually this involves students completing six hours worth of experiments. Most people decide to leave this until the last few weeks of school... Do yourself a favor and knock these out early on when you have nothing else to do. Also, it's worthwhile to sign up for a 2-hour experiment since many end early. As for specific courses, some favorite are Social Gerontology, Developmental Psych and Abnormal Psych.

Though some of the Wash. U. community might view the psychology major as a bit of a joke since exams are relatively easy and coursework is light, this should not be a deterrent for anyone invested in the material (even if he or she has no desire to go into the field post-grad). Instead, my recommendation would be to enjoy the psychology major for all of its benefits and interesting information and to look into completing a second major alongside it.

English

Your eyes are bloodshot. Your fingers are numb. Your brain feels like honeydew with all of the sweet stuff scooped out. You remind yourself that there are only three days left to finish the thirty-plus pages of writing due at the end of the semester. You are stuck on page seven, rewriting the same insipid sentence that should be the catalyst of your thesis on Joseph Conrad's utilization of impressionistic imagery to illustrate the nihilism in The Heart of Darkness. A scoop of that honeydew would taste really good right about now, oh "The horror! The horror!"

However, as the semester subsides and you make all your deadlines, a feeling of accomplishment overtakes you. This period of arduous work is put into perspective, as you realize that until finals your workload was merely readings and few short papers. These readings consisted of not only literature and poetry, but also a wide variety of excerpts from across academia. Ranging from psychology, history, philosophy, sociology, and even the hard sciences, the English major takes these seemingly mutually exclusive disciplines and synthesizes them through the common thread of art. If this multifaceted education is appealing, English major is for you, as you will study both the intellectual and emotional human experience through the power of the written word.

Accordingly, as an English major at Wash. U., your work will not only be scrutinized for strength of your logical and literary analysis, but also style and mechanics. This demand is greater than your peers studying other disciplines whose work is graded neither for mechanics nor style. However, the fruits of your labor are great as an ability to write clearly and grammatically correct is an increasingly lost skill. Many students, moreover, who have a specific interest in the function of style in the creative writing process pursue the Writing Minor. Taking courses such as "Fiction Writing" and "Creative Non-Fiction", these students learn techniques to document their personal experiences and make their innate creativity into an art form.

However, as you are writing a sonnet for your "Poetry Writing" course beneath that stunning tree in the quad, one of your peers asks you the adage question, "What are you going to do with an English major?" At a pre-professional school like Wash. U. majoring in English might seem to be quite shortsighted. To many it seems that you are relishing in academia, instead of learning skills to survive in the 'real world'. Although the English major (outside of writing clear and logically) does not offer the hard skills of other majors, it gives students many intangible skills stemming from being well read. These skills include the ability to communicate clearly, recognize perceptions, and critically analyze situations. Consequently, many English major's study pre-law,

33

Academics

have second business majors, and even are even seen carrying MCAT textbooks next to Shakespeare.

So if you crave the nuances of life, desiring an abstract, artistic, and intellectual college experience that will not leave you at loss in the future, the English major is just for you.

... and 3 You Don't

PNP

Philosophy-Neuroscience-Psychology (PNP) is literally the headiest major at Wash. U. As a PNP major, you will have the opportunity to engage in highly interrelated tridisciplinary studies without burdening yourself with multiple majors and minors. PNP majors often describe their studies as a quest to understand what it means to think (philosophy), how we think (neuroscience), and what our thoughts mean (psychology). As a PNP major, you will truly gain profound insight into the mind-body problem, or more simply, how we can reconcile our first-person, unique conscious psychological experience with the fundamental aspects of the physical world.

In general, PNP is not considered an easy major, but with its psych-heavy requirements it is certainly not as difficult as an engineering or architecture degree. As a Freshman, you can enroll in the Mind, Brain, and Behavior seminar track, which allows you to skip a few intro classes that are fairly boring (Intro/Inquiry in the Cognitive Sciences). The two general tracks in PNP are LCC (language, culture and cognition) and CN (cognitive neuroscience). Almost 90% of all PNP majors choose the CN tract, although students who are interested in psychology and the mind-brain but less scientifically inclined may choose the LCC tract, which replaces neurosciences depth requirements with linguistic and anthropology courses.

Within either tract there is a large amount of room of customization – as long as you take enough credits within each category (psychology, neuroscience/linguistics/anthro, philosophy) you are free to choose any class you find interesting. For example, if you are interested in language, you can take Philosophy of Language, Psychology of Language, and multiple linguistics courses. In terms of specific class recommendations, it really comes down to your particular interests. The PNP department does a fairly good job putting together interesting course listings every semester, although beware: many classes are not offered on a yearly basis!

So why become a PNP major? Besides acquiring the ability to initiate amazingly intriguing conversations at cocktail parties, you will also learn to approach problems from multiple perspectives. You will

Academics

gain profound perspective on the mind-body problem. Not only will you will set yourself up for success in any psychological, philosophical, or cognitive neuroscience research, but you will also be a strong candidate for many jobs that require critical thinking and problem solving – you are trying to tackle the ultimate question about the human conscious experience!

Urban Studies

Urban studies is a small, but quickly growing major; it works best for students who aim to be in the social sciences professionally. The major is outlined to make students marketable graduate school applican'ts by ideally taking the core course, Studying the City, sophomore year, going abroad (in Capetown, South Africa, at Oxford in England, or Washington, DC) and completing an internship junior year to prep for writing a senior thesis. It is a rigorous major where students cannot shy away into anonymous-number status; small numbers permit strong faculty support to help students set and reach high goals.

Almost any course that falls under public health, political science, education, international studies, or psychology can count towards your urban studies major, so you get out what you put in for this major. You can be an anonymous student graded by multiple choice tests and papers in International Public Health, or a member of small discussion-based classes like Sociology for Education. The knowledge and skills that you gain from each course definitely contribute to your performance in other classes, but prior class knowledge is certainly not required for you do well, so you can jump around in upper and lower level courses to follow your interests without needing any prerequisites.

The Study of Cities, the only required course besides Stats2100, functions as a weed out course and requires a lot of reading and a big group project. The workload and classroom vibe can be intimidating, but provides a great opportunity for students to learn more than they ever thought existed about urban issues. The students who thrive are those who are able to suck it up and use the intimidation as an incentive to prove themselves.

Although faculty-student attention is dwindling as more students enroll in the major, professors are still eager to guide and to support the students with similar interests who will work hard. For example, aside from the core course and Stats2100, all urban studies majors are required to write a senior thesis. If you're GPA is below 3.5, then you write a thesis in the fall semester of senior year. It can be a lot of work, but Prof. Yeakey, the director of the urban studies department, makes a point to be accessible to students during the process. If students don't take initiative, they will not get more than a piece of paper with thesis guidelines at the beginning of the year, but if they put in the effort they will find help at every corner.

Environmental Studies

If you're looking for a major that will send you headfirst into thinking critically about how to solve many of the major problems of modern society (or if you're a hippy), look no further than environmental studies. In your classes, you might learn about genetic engineering, eco-villages, and the mating behavior of bees. But it's not all "love and peace, man." You can choose between the ecology and geosciences track, or the social sciences track. The ecology track involves a lot of science and theory based classes, while the social sciences track involve, well, more social sciences courses, and are aimed at students who want to go into environmental policy.

Environmental studies is a major that is very flexible and allows you to study what you want in many different departments. This has led people to refer to the major as a joke and, in some cases, this is admittedly true. Because there is such a variety of classes to choose from, some students decide to take courses in philosophy, chemistry, and anthropology classes without trying to find any common theme to tie them together. Though these students will always exist, this year the major was changed so that you can't just take a random assortment of classes (i.e. all the easy ones) and call yourself a Wash. U. graduate. Now, the curriculum is more organized and taken more seriously within the university. If you are interested in ecology, there are also tons of opportunities to do research. Doing research is a great way to get some lab work in if you plan on being a scientist when you graduate, but even if you aren't you'll also have the chance to go hiking outdoors, play with frogs in ponds, and still have enough time to go out every Thursday.

Pre-Med Survival Guide
YOU CAN DO THIS!

Before reading this, write down why you want to be a doctor. Take this seriously. Done? Don't lose this. This paper is your metaphorical drive that many students quickly lose, especially once they get into the heat of battle with the Wash. U. pre-med curriculum. One thing you must absolutely remember is the following mantra:

If you truly want to become a doctor, you will.

I'll get back to that later. Now let me throw some startling numbers your way. While I can in no way attest to their empirical accuracy, as a pre-med kid who has been through it all, I'm confident they are concrete ballpark figures. Let's assume the incoming class is 1,500 students. On average, around 700 of these students will be pre-med, or just under half. Once the first Chem 111 exam is returned (about the third week in September) this number will probably drop to 600. By the end of the first semester, this number will probably drop a bit more. Those who survive will likely enroll in Bio 2960. After the end of Freshman year, it is probably a safe bet that the number of pre-meds in the class will be about 400. By the end of the first semester of Organic Chemistry – if not by the 3rd test – this number will probably drop to 100, which is around the number that usually applies in each class.

What did you say? Weed out? While this may be the rumor, I can honestly say I do not think Wash. U. intentionally weeds out with the goal of boosting the statistics of their applican'ts. Sure, the classes are extremely scary. Yes, the classes are scaled. Yes, the average score on most of the Chem 111, Bio 2960, and Orgo tests will be in the 60s. Yes, you will have to study more than you ever have in order to get an A, or even a B-. That being said, don't be intimidated. I must reiterate:

If you truly want to become a doctor, you will.

Here are 5 great tips to help you excel during the first year of pre-med classes:

1) ***Join a PLTL.*** This stands for peer-led team-learning. While this will be explained more thoroughly to you during your first few classes, the idea is that you meet for two hours outside of class every week with a mentor (who received an A in the class) and a

group of less than 8 other students. During this session you work on problems that aren't available outside of the program and that are extremely beneficial to performing well on the tests. It may also be a nice opportunity to meet some fellow students who share similar interests.

2) ***Keep up with the work.*** One of the most important things throughout this journey – and it certainly is a journey – is to stay sane. If you leave yourself with too much on your plate at once, you will create unnecessary, preventable stress and drop out for the wrong reasons. It is easy to skip classes and wait until the last second to study for exams (been there, done that) but believe me, you want to do a little bit of work often rather than a lot at once.

3) ***For god sakes, stay social!*** While I think a certain level of stress is necessary in order to keep the drive alive, everyone needs to have some fun in college. I'm not saying you need to make Tuesday and Thursday study nights and reserve the rest of the days for going out to bars, but you should work on your time management from the start. Figure out a system that works for you and make it happen. There will be times when your academic schedule conflicts with your social agenda – these situations are difficult, but you have to keep your priorities in mind. Believe me, it can be tough, but keep your eye on the prize.

4) ***Meet with a Pre-Health adviser early on.*** The advising system the school provides is a tremendous resource – don't be afraid to use it from the beginning to get some sense of direction. That being said, do not let them intimidate you. Many people will not get above a B in many of the pre-med classes, and advisors may tell you to either get your grades up or call it quits. Once again, if you truly want to be come a doctor, you will. I know of someone who didn't do tremendously as an undergraduate, went to medical school in the Caribbean, and now he is the Chief Resident of Trauma Surgery at Vanderbilt. Believe me, if the drive is there, you will make it.

5) ***Don't overextend.*** While it is important – not only for your resume but also for your sanity – to have some extra-curriculars outside of your rigorous academic life, don't overdo it. You don't have to be a leader of 12 different groups and a published author

Academics

in Nature by the time you apply your junior or senior year. You simply need to show the admissions committees that you are passionate and driven. That's it.

If you heed my advice and repeat the mantra in your head, you will come out of your first year relatively unscathed, but this doesn't mean you can start slacking off. Here are five important things to keep in mind as you journey on:

1) *Consider taking a class over the summer*. As you may have noticed from the introduction or heard from other students, organic chemistry and Wash. U. are bitches. The first semester isn't terrible if you are good with chemicals (I'm not talking about Adderall, don't start taking Adderall. Coffee is fine.) But, in order to get above a B in either semester, especially the second, you will probably have to study no less than 30 hours for each test, not including class hours. My best advice – make life easy and take Orgo at a local school. While this may not sound like something schools will find as appealing as the Wash. U. Orgo credit stamp, less stress during the school year seems, at least to me, to be infinitely more beneficial to your overall happiness as a pre-med student at Wash. U.

2) *Shadow doctors, immerse yourself in hospital life*. Many schools emphasize previous time in a clinical setting. MEDPREP, a course that will soon be required of all pre-med students, allows students to shadow emergency medicine residents at Barnes-Jewish-Childrens (BJC), the Wash. U. teaching hospital. While this is certainly a great start, it is important to try and go above and beyond this experience. Try and network at home to see if anyone's parents or friends are physicians and would be willing to let you shadow them for a day. This can sometimes be an intimidating endeavor, but I promise it will be a worthwhile experience for both you and your resume.

3) *Plan a time to take the MCAT*. If you've read this far you clearly care enough about becoming a doctor to realize the MCAT is a serious part of the application process. Wash. U. offers a fabulous prep course that provides students with some of the best study materials (Exam Kracker prep books) as well as lectures and access to all of the official AAMC practices tests. You should plan on finishing all of your pre-reqs before taking the MCAT, and I'd recommend enrolling in the Wash. U. prep course before taking the exam. Also, if you plan

on taking your MCAT during the year, take a light courseload ! **YOU SHOULD SPEND AT LEAST 6 WEEKS STUDYING FOR THE MCAT** if you want to achieve a competitive score. The more you study, the better you will do.

4) *Study something you are interested in besides biology*. If biology is absolutely your favorite subject then by all means, be a bio major. But keep in mind that you'll only be an undergraduate once – live it up! There's absolutely no reason to streamline yourself this early if you've always loved Shakespeare or Stalin or Socrates. Major in something you will enjoy spending four years learning. Take the bio classes that interest you. And that you can do well in.

5) *Get to know your professors*. Once you get into some more interesting, higher-level classes, you are bound to connect with your professors. Introduce yourself early in the semester. Ask questions after class, explore and expand on the material. Sound like bullshit? Maybe it is, but this isn't high school: you need to make the extra effort to get to know your teachers. Not only will this be crucial for obtaining good recommendations, but it will really make a good class great.

(Somewhat) Easier Classes to Help Boost the Science GPA
*Endocrinology
*Human Physiology
*Orgo III
*Nutrition (U-College)
*Stars and Galaxies
*Problem-Based Learning in the Biomedical Sciences
Others can be found in the Pre-health office, located in Umrath Hall.

REMEMBER, IF YOU TRULY WANT TO BECOME A DOCTOR, YOU WILL

Academics

Top 10

Places to Get Your Study On

10: South Forty Study Rooms

9: The DUC

8: Olin Library Reading Room

7: East Asian Library

6: Whispers Café

5: Brookings Quad on a nice day

4: Olin Library Level 1

3: Art School Library

2: Law School Library

1: Any toilet (Two birds, one stone)

Being Pre-Law

Being pre-law is like declaring a major, except easier, you don't have to declare. If someone says they are "pre-law" what they really mean is that they have the intention of going to law school. There are no requirements for being pre-law, and if someone told you there were certain classes you need to take to take for law school, they would be wrong. However, just because there are no requirements doesn't mean there aren't things you can do that will make the application process easier. Here are a few tips that I wish I had known before going through the process:

Choose a pre-law advisor
There are three pre-law advisors that will help you through the process of preparing for and getting into law school. Building a relationship with them early on will make everything much easier. Also, by contacting one of them you will be put on a pre-law mailing list that will send you periodic updates about where you should be in the process.

Professor recommendations
You will need at least two recommendations from professors, and it's nice to get them from those who know you best. Start thinking about this your sophomore year, and build relationships with professors that allow them to get to know you outside of class. Try to avoid getting recommendations from freshman year professors.

Get legal-related internships over the summers
I cannot tell you how many lawyers have told me to not go to law school. The reason is because they have seen so many people go without knowing that it's what they really want, and later realize it wasn't for them. Get an internship over the summer so you can get a peek into the life of a lawyer. It will also look good on your application.

Have a few informational interviews
This is a great way to get a better understanding of specific types of law, and it builds your network for connections in the future. If you fall in love with one kind of law, you may want to consider schools that have a particularly strong department in that area.

Academics

Start studying early for the LSAT
It's a tough test, and the best way to get better is to practice. Start early, minimize the pressure, and put in fewer hours per day over a long period of time rather than many hours per day in a short time. Cramming doesn't work for this test.

Take some legal studies or political science classes
While there may not be specific requirements, there are classes that relate to the law and may give insight as to what legal classes are like. At the very least you'll see some material that will undoubtedly reappear in law school.

Wash. U.phamisms

5) Gargoyle- p., Concert venue in the Mallinkrodt center that hosts great indie bands throughout the semester. In 2007 a Girl-Talk concert was cut short when a drunk senior got naked and was subsequently tazed by WUPD.
6) Bowles Plaza - p., This large courtyard on the backside of Mallinkrodt plays host to the ArtSci happy hour. Its open space and theater seating makes it an ideal venue for other student events, or even a place for students to grab a seat and have lunch on a nice day.

Doing Research

So you chose a major and you like it enough to get more involved? Need a good recommendation, want to spice up that CV or earn honors? How about making a little extra cash or getting some easy credits? If you said yes to any of the above, then research may be a good idea for you.

Undergraduate research at Wash. U. takes on many forms. In the natural sciences and engineering fields you'll probably find yourself with pipettes, Bunsen burners and lab coats. If you do social sciences or humanities research, you'll find yourself with a mountain of books in Olin or maybe even the comfort of your own bed. But no matter what field you choose, the first question to ask is: what will you study?

Each department has its own way of doing things, but the easiest way to find a project is to talk to a professor that you like or that works on something that interests you. Approach the professor directly, indicate your interest to work with them and ask to find out more about their research. If all goes well, they'll give you a stack of papers and the research begins. Your level of involvement (and amount of pay or credits earned) will depend on your availability, your skill set and your desire to actually get work done. If possible, devote a summer to a specific project; working full-time is when you truly learn how to conduct research. In the case that your professor can't afford to pay you or you are working independently, the Career Center, the Office of Undergraduate Research or your department may have grants available to support your work.

A rewarding aspect of undergraduate research is being recognized for your work. The Office of Undergraduate Research has a research journal and a research symposium each semester where student researchers can present their work. Many departments require that you complete an undergraduate thesis to earn honors, which is a pain to write, but also one of the most gratifying experiences of college. Finally, if you get lucky (or are actually good at what you do), your research can be published in a peer-reviewed journal.

Some practical words of advice: Be honest with the people that you work with and never be afraid to ask questions. It's much better to look stupid and get it right the first time than to screw up and break an expensive piece of equipment or waste someone's time.

And if you don't want to do the research but still want to be involved, the psych department always needs human lab rats (really).

Academics

Study Abroad

Preparation

The first piece of advice that can be given to someone thinking of going abroad is that you should. Now, there are many reasons why people cannot go, but also many excuses. If you think you're not going because of an excuse, you should be sending in an application and hopping on a plane.

Once you've decided to go abroad, the question becomes where to go. For some people this decision may be made much easier based on the options available for your major or minor. But no matter how many options your major offers, there is a good chance that there are language requirements for a many of the destinations, meaning you need to speak the native language with a certain level of proficiency to study there. The level varies from program to program, but if you know you want to go abroad to a certain country, make sure you begin fulfilling the language requirements early on. If not, you may find your dream location just out of reach. On the other hand, some schools in countries that speak foreign languages do not require you to speak their language, including France and the Czech Republic, but it's good to be prepared anyway.

Another thing that needs to be taken into account is how many credits you can get while you're abroad. In some cases, you may need to take summer courses or heavier loads the semesters before or after if you really want to go. In addition to credits, you need to check when certain required classes are offered. If they're only offered the semester that you're planning to go abroad, make sure to get them done the year before so you don't have to worry about it senior year.

As a last resort, and if you have enough credits, you have the option of taking the semester off and going pretty much anywhere, for much, much cheaper. If you go down this route you will apply directly to the foreign schools instead of through WashU, and the classes won't count towards your graduation requirements.

One option that many people don't even consider is going abroad during the fall semester because such a high number of students go during the spring. However, there are a few reasons to go abroad first semester. One of the biggest is that if you have older friends, you will be able to spend their last semester with them before they go off into the real world. Second semester also has a lot of events, such as Thurtene,

46

that you don't want to miss. You will also have a much easier time getting jobs and internships, which usually recruit during the spring semester.

Being Abroad

See as much as you can see, do as much as you can do, and most important of all, meet as many people as you can meet. This is one of the greatest opportunities of your life, don't let it pass you by. Meeting people from other parts of the world is one of the most eye-opening and enlightening experiences you can have. Ask people about their pasts, their families, their country and its politics, their favorite music, whatever. If you are on a program with a lot of people from Wash. U. it will be tempting to only hang out with them, but don't fall into the trap. It's fine to have friends from Wash. U., but you will be missing out on something huge if you don't reach out of your comfort zone and meet some new people.

Grad School Preparation

Now that you've been accepted to college, it's time to start thinking about graduation. There are hundreds of options open to you once you graduate, and it's important to plan ahead. While it's nothing to be worried about, post graduation plans are a good thing to keep in mind. One of the options many people choose is to go to graduate school. Graduate school is a great way to get more involved in a subject you love and a great way to open new doors and advance your career.

Wash. U. has a great Pre-Grad program that has a lot of information about preparing and getting into graduate school. Speaking to advisors, reading their online material, and attending Pre-Grad seminars are all useful ways to learn about graduate school. Taking more than one class with a certain professor you like or signing up for small classes are both ways to get to know professors who can give you advice about grad schools and hopefully write you recommendations. Exploring subjects at a greater depth than required is the best way to find your passions. Going past the minimum number of credits for your major or minor gives you a better idea of what the subject is all about, and will also allow you to take more advanced classes at the start of graduate school.

Relevant experience outside of the classroom is also very important. Options include working in a lab, helping a professor with research, or writing a senior thesis. If you are able to get an internship in the field you're interested in, even better. Assistant Dean and PreGrad Advisor Cathleen Fleck notes, "Some doctoral programs especially will not even consider you if you have not had a significan't research experience before applying." And in addition to increasing the strength of your application, you will also be learning if a graduate school setting is right for you.

If you decide you do want to go to grad school, you will begin a process very different from choosing an undergraduate university. The biggest difference is that because your interests have narrowed down a bit, you need to look for a school that is the best at exactly what you want. This is not always easy. Dean Fleck says, "Considering what you want in a graduate school program is sometimes hard until you start to look at the options available. Some sample questions are: What courses are offered? Do they help you with gaining practical experience?

Do I write a thesis and when? Where do the graduates get jobs? What funding options are there? Take note that, for certain professional Master's programs, at least two years' experience is recommended, if not required. For many PhD programs, you can enter straight out of undergraduate school, with the assumption that you will do work equivalent to a Master's along the way to a PhD. Again, look at websites and ask around for these answers." Another important difference to note is that it is not uncommon to find a stellar PhD program at a less than stellar university. To find out which schools are the best you should talk to professors, advisors, parents, and check out published ranking and grad school guides.

If you are worried about paying for grad school, you have a few options. Most PhD programs will cover the cost of tuition and provide a stipend as well. This is less likely for Master's programs, so you will probably have better luck looking for scholarships or taking out a student loan.

Lastly, you will need to know what grad schools are looking for in a candidate. According to Dean Fleck these factors are:
1) Relevant Experience
2) References/Recommendation letters (usually 3 required)
3) Application Essay: also called Personal Statement / Statement of Purpose
4) Standardized Exams (GRE or GMAT)
5) Transcripts
6) Academic Writing or Research Sample (not as necessary for Master's programs)

For more information contact Dean Cathleen Fleck, PhD, Pregrad Advisor, College of Arts & Sciences (pregrad@artsci.wustl.edu) or Amy Heath Carpentier, MA, Career Specialist, The Career Center (heath-carpentier@wustl.edu). You can also check their website at http://college.artsci.wustl.edu/pregrad, and join the Pre-Grad mailing list by sending an email to pregrad@artsci.wustl.edu.

*Special thanks to Dean Fleck for providing us with the information for this article.

Academics

Career Center

One of the most useful yet underutilized resources Wash. U. has to offer is the Career Center. Conveniently located in the DUC and open Monday thru Friday from 8:30 a.m. till 5 p.m., the Career Center is a place that students should get acquainted with early on in their college careers.

Most students come to the Career Center for one-on-one advising with the Career Center staff, who come from various academic and professional fields. The advisors can help students with internship/job searches, resume/cover letter reviews, and mock interviews. In addition to one-on-one advising, the Career Center puts on an array of events from workshops and panel reviews, to networking events. If you are totally lost as to what you want to do in the future (and most people are), the center offers self-assessment tools such as MBTI, StrengthsQuest, Strong Interest Inventory and Elevations. Lastly the center provides envelopes and resume papers, free printing for career related materials, and a library of magazines, industry guides, and interview manuals that you can read or make copies of.

Going to the Career Center does not mean that they are going to find you a job or magically solve your problems, but it can be a huge help. Most students don't use the career center until the last minute senior year, but the more familiar you are with the Career Center, the more useful it will be. Spending time getting to know the career advisors and familiarizing yourself with the center will be invaluable when the time comes for you to find an internship or a job. It's never too early to start exploring your passions and career opportunities.

III

Wash. U.
Preparing for School

I grew up below the poverty line; I didn't have as much as other people did. I think it made me stronger as a person, it built my character. Now I have a 4.0 grade point average and I want to go to college, and just become a better person.

-Justin Bieber

Things to Consider
For your first day

Check in:
Arrive as early as possible. Move-in is one of the few times that cars are allowed to drive onto the 40, but if you don't snatch a spot early you will be waiting around with your parents for quite a while. If you have your own dolly, bring it. Although the school will have some available for use, they are a hot commodity and hard to come by.

Getting your stuff to school:
The best way to bring your belongings to school is by driving. Of course, this is not an option for everyone. If you are taking a plane, make sure your parents pack light and shove all of your stuff into their bags so you don't get slammed with extra baggage fees. You may also think of using the student-run company UTrucking, which will pick up your stuff from your home (or home area) and bring it to school, although there is a hefty price tag attached. Lastly, you can just buy everything when you arrive in St. Louis. Bed, Bath, & Beyond has a great registry program where you can scour your hometown store with a scanner and pick out everything you want for your dorm. That information will then be sent to the St. Louis branch, and everything that you want will be waiting in a neat bundle for you on the day you arrive. I'd recommend overscanning initially as you can elect to remove items when you actually arrive at the St. Louis branch, and items tend to go quickly if you don't have them reserved.

Television:
You need one, but you don't need two. Talk with your roommate and decide who will bring the TV. Make sure you have a DVD player and/or video game system as well. You will be playing more video games than you ever thought possible. N64 with Super Smash Bros. will make you the coolest kid on your floor, and you can't get a DUI for playing Mario Kart drunk.

Computer:
Every college student has a Mac. Do you want to be cool?

Music:
Make sure you have an external hard drive for your music, and speakers if you plan on hosting hang out sessions in your room (your dinky computer speakers won't cut it). Having an external hard drive is a great way to share music with other students, and expand your library. If you're from the

northeast, you should quickly seek out some southerners and download some good ol' fashion country music.

Money:
The local bank on campus is Bank of America, so you will want to open an account with them. They have multiple ATM's and a banking center where you can deposit money or deal with any money issues you may have. You might also want to consider purchasing a Bear Card, produced by a student run company, which gives you discounts at many St. Louis locations. Many people purchase the card and then never use it, but if you don't fall into this trap, it is well worth it.

Phone:
Pretty much any major wireless provider will have service on campus, but Verizon seems to have the best overall coverage. That being said, don't expect to have good service inside your dorm, no matter how good your map is.

Food:
When you get accepted to Wash. U., you will be forced to buy a meal plan. The best option is to buy the cheapest plan you can. When you buy your initial plan, one point is not equal to one dollar; it is actually equal to a little less. Dollars have a bad exchange rate with meal points. This means that you are paying more money than the food is actually worth. If your meal points run out, you can purchase more at a one-to-one rate. This is a trap that everyone falls into. Don't make this mistake. You will also want to go out and purchase food from Schnucks (the local grocery store), Target, Trader Joe's, Walmart, Sam's club or Costco if you are a member. Stock up while your parents are there. Food sold in stores on campus is much more expensive than the food you find in the aforementioned locations.

Transportation:
Freshman cannot bring cars to campus, so if you plan on traveling off campus, it's a good idea to make friends with upperclassmen. However, the St. Louis Metro can get you to most places you want to go in St. Louis. Make sure you sign up for a U-Pass which lets you ride the metro for free. Don't forget this. Campus is easy to navigate on foot, but you might want to get a bike if you are frequently late to things, or if you want to get off campus without relying on other people. Bikes can be found on Craigslist, at Walmart, or for rent by the on-campus company Bears Bikes. Although not necessary, a bike is certainly a worthwhile investment for the next four years.

Preparations

Meeting People:
Don't be shy. Talk to as many people as you can. You will forget every single one of their names, but don't worry because they will forget your name too. If you are moved-in, offer to help other people on your floor. Eat meals at tables with other people and introduce yourself. Go to at least your first floor meeting. Maybe.

Buying books:
The bookstore will carry the text books for almost all of your classes, but you can always find them cheaper online. Also, there are many classes where a "required text" isn't necessary to do well in the course. Don't rush to buy your books until you are certain that you can't get by without them. Another good option is to buy your books online from websites like Amazon or half.com, which are cheaper options than the book store.

Editor's Tip: Don't feel like you have to buy everything before you get to school. You really won't know what you will need or want in your room until you get a feel for the place. Don't rush, calm down, and realize that you can get everything you need in the first weeks of school. Just make sure you have enough to survive the days you are moving in.

Picking Classes

Picking classes at Wash. U. is an art, and we happen to be quite gifted when it comes to crafting a perfect schedule. Over the course of eight semesters, every student finds his or her own way of getting the process down, but we want to give you some tips so that you can come up with your game plan earlier those students who don't have this book. Aside from school and major requirements, you are going to want to consider a number of other things as you construct your school-week.

Start looking at class options early
The school posts the class listings online many weeks before registration begins. Use the registration worksheet on WebSTAC and throw classes on there that look interesting. It's surprisingly easy to forget the name of certain class that looks interesting and never end up finding it again.

Give yourself some electives, but not too many
It's really nice to give yourself a chance to try classes that aren't required, but make sure you spend time getting requirements done early in your Wash. U. career. The last thing you want is to be stuck with a semester's worth of requirements the semester before graduation. Typically, 1-2 electives is appropriate for a 5-6 class course load.

Think about how social you want to be and when
If you are the type of person that likes to go out Thursday nights, don't plan classes late Thursday or early Friday. If you want to do research or work a job, try to fit these into your schedule. Also consider the size of the class—if it's small, chances are you won't be able to skip it those mornings you feel like you just got hit by a train. Consider these issues on a larger time scale as well—you may want to give yourself an easier senior year by loading up on credits Freshman and Sophomore years.

Talk to people who have been there before
Older friends, older brothers and sisters, older brothers and sisters of friends, older friends of brothers and sisters—really anyone that can give you some insight into which classes are the right ones to take. What every student will tell you is that it's not about the class as much as it is about the teacher. It's often the teacher that really ignites your passion for a subject, not the material itself. Checking out past evaluations through course listings is a great way to get a feel for how the class

Preparations

operated in previous semesters. People that have been there before will be able to tell you whom to take classes from, even if they haven't taken a specific class before.

If you want it easy don't do it alone, coordinate with friends
It's much easier to do well in a class when you have a friend by your side. Many classes meet at multiple times, so it's often possible to find a class that works for both of you. However, many of the classes you'll take won't be filled with your floormates, so be prepared to make friends in class so you don't find yourself alone when the procrastination panic during finals kicks in.

Sign up for 7 classes, always!
Usually students will take 5 or 6 classes a semester, but there is no reason for you not to start with 7 and then drop as many as you want during the shopping period. Even if you think you know what you want, it's worth checking out some other possibilities because you may be surprised what you fall in love with.

Start every semester with one class as pass/fail
You shouldn't take more than 2 or 3 pass/fail classes over the course of your 4 years, but it's worth starting the semester off with what you think your hardest (non-required) class will be as pass/fail. You have weeks into the semester to change the credit type, and you will feel relieved to know the class won't effect your grade when that first midterm doesn't go as planned. In other words: why not? – you have nothing to lose.

Before your registration time, keep an eye on WebSTAC
Some of the classes you planned on taking may already have an 80-person waitlist. If that's the case, don't waste one of your 7 classes on that one and go for something else, it's not going to happen. On the other hand, depending on the size of the class, some professors will decide to teach another section or take in some people on the waitlist. As a general rule, if you're under 30 in a large lecture class, or under 15 in a smaller class, stay on the list. And when you are on the watilist, email the professor explaining why you want to take their class if it's really important to you. They will often let you in if you make a little extra effort.

- Set your alarm clock: Some registrations are early, don't miss yours!

Cornerstone
The Center for Advanced Learning

Wash. U.'s Cornerstone center serves the student body in many ways. Cornerstone supplies resources for Wash. U. students with disabilities, provides tutoring and team learning programs, offers writing help and advice through its writing center, and gives dedicated students the opportunity to make money by simply taking good notes. The Cornerstone office is located on the South Forty, very close to all of the underclassmen dorms so it is convenient to take advantage of all the services that Cornerstone offers. All services are offered to students free of charge.

Resources for Students With Disabilities

Do you have a learning disability, ADHD, or dyslexia? If so, then Cornerstone is the Wash. U. institution that will accommodate your learning needs. A professional from Cornerstone meets with every Wash. U. student with disabilities and develops a plan to accommodate each individual student based on his/her own abilities. Cornerstone provides areas for students with disabilities to take exams in quiet areas that are free from distraction. Additionally, they provide note-taking services for students who cannot take notes in class for whatever (legitimate) reason, or for whom English is a second language. The services for students that Cornerstone provides are an incredible resource for students with disabilities and enable those students to have an equal footing with all other Wash. U. undergraduates.

Tutoring and Peer-Learning Programs

In addition to providing services to students with disabilities, Cornerstone also provides valuable assistance to the general Wash. U.student body. Cornerstone pays academically successful upperclassmen to provide one-on-one and group tutoring sessions to students in many subjects such as chemistry, calculus and physics. In addition to tutoring, Cornerstone facilitates Peer-Led Team Learning (PLTL) programs that are designed to help students enrolled in large, difficult, science and math classes help each other learn the material. Cornerstone fosters a collaborative atmosphere in which students want to help other students to succeed.

Preparations

The Cornerstone Writing Center

Cornerstone also provides a Writing Center, where proven upperclassmen writers will read and edit other students' papers for free! Advice from Writing Center staff is an amazing resource and has been proven to improve the grades of students who utilize this service.

Want a Job? Go to Cornerstone

Where do all of these amazing services that Cornerstone offers come from? Many of them are provided by dedicated students who get paid to run the Cornerstone programs. Dedicated undergraduate students are paid competitive wages to tutor, lead peer-led study sessions, and even simply take notes for classes in which they are enrolled. If you want to get a job that pays well and enables you to help other students at the same time, then take advantage of the jobs offered by Wash. U.'s Cornerstone Center for Advanced Learning!

Private Music Lessons
A chance to get out of the library

When talking about Wash. U. with friends from other colleges, nobody gets jealous about our always-packed library, the decent food offerings, or our bi-annual attempts at throwing a good concert. However, if you mention that our school offers private musical instrument lessons for credit, people go wild. Wash. U. offers private lessons for just about every standard instrument and some unusual ones including the lute, harpsichord, harmonica, and banjo.

Semester options include ½ hour/week for 1.5 credits, or 1 hour/week for 3 credits. That's right, just one hour a week, and you can get yourself 3 credits towards graduation and your GPA. While an A is not automatic, a modest level of effort is enough to keep most teachers happy. It will certainly be less effort than getting an A in your 400-level 3-credit economics course. Nonetheless, make sure to read the fine print as the music department has certain limits to how much private lesson credits one can receive.

As for the lessons themselves, don't worry if you are a beginner just trying to pick out your first guitar chords or an experienced jazz pianist; the music department has teachers for all levels. In regards to musical style, the department has clear focuses on jazz and classical. But don't be discouraged if you want to learn pop or rock. The key here is to do some background research on the teachers. Chances are you have a friend who knows which teacher is a hard-ass, which teacher is flexible, which teacher ate roast beef, and which teacher ate none.

Many of the musicians on staff are world-class and it is worth getting to spend some up-close and personal time with them. Naturally, this offering goes beyond the standard tuition, and costs an additional several hundred dollars per semester. Nevertheless, any budding musician should take advantage of this opportunity to learn from a master musician (and get 3 GPA-friendly credits) for several semesters.

Freshman Housing

Matriculating freshmen at Wash. U. have limited housing options on their admissions forms: modern or traditional; single, double, or triple; substance-free or not. The Residential Life Office assigns students, according to their preferences, to various freshmen-only buildings on the South 40 acres of campus (referred to as the South 40). The buildings the office chooses to house freshmen and sophomores can change from year to year, but generally, the following buildings comprise the primary residences of first-year students. Here is a brief description of each:

Traditional

These dorms are known for being more social, but also grungier. Residents use communal bathrooms, one for males and one for females on each floor.

Lee

A "riot-proof" building style makes for angular, maze-like hallways in Lee. A kitchen and common room with a balcony on each floor provide areas for socializing.

Beaumont

Like Lee, Beaumont features riot-proof hallways. This building, however, does not have common rooms on each floor. Its bottom floor contains larger gathering areas and a kitchen but no residential rooms.

Rubelmann

Rubelmann is the only traditional dorm with straight hallways. Wash. U. plans to renovate the building soon, updating it to mirror the architecture of Umrath and the South 40 House complex nearby.

Modern

These dorms are newer than traditional. A private bathroom may connect two double rooms or sit within "suites" which comprise either two double rooms or four single rooms.

Park

Park sits at the back of the South 40 and overlooks the Swamp, a large field in the middle of the dorms. Park is known for large, spaced-out suites, but some students complain about the bent hallways dividing the hall socially.

Eliot A

Eliot A houses one room that ResLife converted to a massage room. On Wednesdays and Thursdays, students can schedule hour-long massages through the fitness center.

Danforth

One floor generally houses Danforth Scholars, a group of freshmen honored by the school for academic performance. Bent hallways sometimes socially divide the halls.

Koenig

The building, sometimes called "Koenig Castle," features turrets that enhance its majestic appearance. Koenig connects to the sophomore dorm, Liggett, and a beautiful wooden library on the first floor provides an ideal study or meeting area.

Umrath

Umrath houses the Congress of the South 40 Office and the Social Justice Center on its entry level. Bear Necessities, a store that sells toiletries and clothing, also sits within the Umrath complex. Some lucky students receive large corner rooms with bay windows.

Dardick

This dorm sits below the intramural athletic fields, and a lawn out front provides an ideal studying and tanning area in good weather.

Lien

Students enjoy the convenience of living here; this is the freshman dorm closest to main campus and allows residents to wake up a few minutes later to get to class on time.

Substance Free Housing

In each residential building there is one floor that is devoted to substance-free ("healthy") living, where students are forced to sign a contract at the beginning of the year stipulating that they will never consume illicit substances on the floor or show up to the floor under the influence at any time. You will have the option of checking a box that reads something along the lines of "would you like to take part in Wash. U.healthy living." For some students this is a great option that allows them to focus on school work at all hours and never have to deal with the distraction of drunken floormates yelling at one another in the middle of the hall. For others, although schoolwork is clearly a priority (you are at Wash. U. after all), it is also important to embrace the social aspects of Wash. U.; this is a university, there will be partying, there will be drinking. As someone who was not on a substance-free floor I can say that drunken people have never directly led to a worse grade, or prevented me from finishing my work. You will also find out that many people who have never drank any alcohol before nonetheless refrain from checking that box, as they want to have as diverse of a floor as possible.

Wash. U.phamisms

7) Art Hill - p., Resting just below the St. Louis Art Museum in Forest Park, Art Hill offers students an ideal place to picnic on a good day. Its views of the park are unparalleled given its location above the paddle boat pond. It's truly the go-to off campus spot on a nice day.

8) The Landing - p., The epicenter of the Thursday night Wash. U. social scene. Offers a wide range of bars right on the river, along with casinos for those bettin' folk.

9) The Clocktower - p., Located across from the new Wohl Center and next to Ursa's, this tall green clock serves as a great location to meet up with friends before heading to campus or out on the town. Cabs will typically come wait around here on weekend nights, and at least one of your friends will try to climb it drunk.

Preparations

Transferring

Transferring schools can be a difficult process. Thankfully, Wash . U. does a great job taking care of its transfer students as they become acclimated to the school. Transfer students undergo an orientation process similar to, but separate from the incoming freshman. Your orientation leaders (known as WUSAs) will be former transfer students themselves, and are a valuable resource. They'll be happy to help you with anything you want to know and will become some of your first friends at Wash. U. Listen to them because they know exactly the position you're in and want to make things as easy for you as possible. Orientation is meant to be fun, so be sure to go to all the events (especially the trip to the City Museum) and try to be as outgoing as possible. Here are many other students who transferred in with you and they probably feel the same way you do. I quickly became friends with a lot of my fellow transfers and ended up living with two of them for both of my years at Wash. U.

One of the problems with transferring is that you'll have missed out on the freshman floor experience, where so many groups of friends

Preparations

are formed. If, like me, you transfer in as a junior, you'll have entirely missed the South 40 experience and may find it difficult to meet new people. This is why it's really important to join clubs, sports teams, student groups, etc. Getting involved will give you a chance to meet people with the same interests as you, and although those transfer friends you made at orientation are great, you're going to want to make friends who have been at Wash. U. since freshman year to show you around.

A big question for a lot of students when they transfer is whether or not to go Greek. Guys have the opportunity to do Fall rush, and between rush and pledge events this will add a lot structure to your social life in your first semester here. Rushing a fraternity is a good way to quickly make some new friends, as you will form a tight bond with your pledge class and the other members of your fraternity. I would only caution that, because you don't have the freshman floor experience to meet other students, you may find that the intense process of pledging isolates you from other people at Wash. U. The students who were here as freshmen and then joined fraternities will have already made other friends on their floors who joined different fraternities or decided not to rush--a luxury transfer students don't have. I personally decided not to join a fraternity, and am happy with my decision, but other kids in my transfer class did join and that decision worked out great for them too.

If you're unsure about it, you can always wait until the Spring and rush then. For girls, a lot of the same pros and cons apply, however, only some sororities take new members in the Fall, and if so it's a pretty informal process. Most of the girls I transferred with who went Greek waited until the Spring to rush and that decision worked out well for a lot of them. The pros and cons about rushing are similar for girls as for guys, except that the pledge process for a sorority is much less intense and takes less time, whereas for guys it's a semester long project.

Academically, you probably won't have the luxury of remaining undeclared for an extended period of time and testing out a bunch of different departments. Do your research on who the good professors are and what the interesting courses are so that you're not wasting your time. Hopefully, you'll be able to jump right into some 300-level courses because of work you did at your last school. These classes will be smaller and will provide a better opportunity to meet people and build relationships with your professors.

As a transfer student, you have the unique perspective of having attended two schools, so try to use that to your advantage. You know what did and didn't work for you at your last school so try to build on that to make your Wash. U. experience as successful as possible.

Wash. U.phamisms:

10) The Underpass - p., The walkway under Forsyth that connects main campus to the South 40. The walls are constantly repainted with advertisements for various student groups and activities on campus. Some think this is a romantic place to stop with their signfican't other on the way back from a party, but we promise you that for every layer of paint there is also a thin coating of Nattified urine along the wall.

11) The Overpass - p., The bridge over Forest Park Parkway connecting the north side of main campus to the main off-campus student neighborhood (U-drive, Kingsbury and Wash Ave). Located behind the main library, this completely caged walkway allows easy access to the loop from main campus.

Preparations

IV

Wash. U.
Living

Cauliflower is nothing but cabbage with a
college education.

-Mark Twain

Schmoozin in St. Louis
The Art of the Schmooooooze

Now that you're in college, I'm going to help you get a job. Let's start from the beginning. Whether you know it or not, we have multiple career centers here at Wash. U., and much of their potential is untapped by the general population. Career Center staff are very knowledgeable, have worked in industries across the board, and are great resources for jump-starting your career. My first piece of advice for students is to set up an appointment with an adviser and simply ask them about the resources they have at their disposal. It is amazing how many resources this school has that no one knows about.

One resource that is particularly helpful is OptimalResume. This is a very simple site that automatically formats what you type into an Olin Business School resume template. It is incredibly easy to use and very helpful if you are having trouble creating a resume. It includes examples, suggested words, different templates for different majors, and help when you can't figure out how to use certain functions. Because the average recruiter will look at your resume for only a few seconds, having a professional looking resume will help you stick out from the rest of the pile.

Other often neglected resources include the classes and trips the Weston Career Center offers for students. When I went on the New York Trek, an annual trip sponsored by the career center that brings you to New York City to meet with different companies, I was at first hesitant as to how valuable it may be. Looking back, the amount of information and knowledge I gained cannot be quantified. Besides networking and getting the business cards of many professionals, it helped me become better versed in professional lingo.

There is also an extensive alumni network in the career center. Alumni are happy to speak with you about their careers and give you advice for your career path. You can look at the database, search for a certain company that you are interested in, and call an alumni that works or has worked for the company and ask for some advice. Who knows, they may like you enough to get you a job. It never hurts to try. Also, reach out and apply to every company you can. Think about it, the worst thing that can happen is that they say no. And you should do your best to get used to it, because you're at Wash. U. and you will be hearing no a lot (I'm not just talking about applications).

Sadly, the phrase "it's not what you know, it's who you know" is quite accurate. You can have all of the necessary skills in the world, but if you are unable to meet and communicate effectively with others, you are shooting yourself in the foot. To get out of the back room and into the corner office you need to be more than smart. The most successful CEO's in the world are those that can communicate with others.

One word of advice is that when you are in a situation where you are networking and speaking with professionals, do NOT ask if they have internships available. It drives people nuts. Be a real person, talk to them about sports, the news, about how much you love the color orange. Literally ANYTHING except asking for internships. It's viewed as rude and deters people from continuing conversation with you. Lastly, make sure you ask for their business card at the end of your meeting.

Another piece of advice when in a networking situation: do your homework. These guys have been working in the industry for years, so if you plan on talking business, politics, science, feelings, etc. know your shit. Don't put yourself in awkward situation by bringing up a topic that you know nothing about. If you are asked a question and you pretend you know but you're wrong, it looks terrible. Answering 'I don't know' is perfectly acceptable as long as it isn't the refrain of your dialogue. Stick to simple conversation; it's much easier, and often more effective. These people know you're in school, so they don't expect you to know everything.

Finally, stay in contact with people you meet. I don't care who it is, send them an email a couple days after saying you enjoyed meeting and speaking with them, and say that you hope to speak with them again in the future. Continuing conversation, although it may seem annoying and over-persistent, is actually a great tool for getting a job in the future. Even if the person works at a company you have no interest in, they may know people in other companies that could help you out. At holiday time, send them a happy holidays note. If you see something about their company in the news, congratulate them. Add them on LinkedIn. Anything that keeps the conversation going, and your name fresh in their memory is a great tool when schmoozing.

The art of the schmooze is not something you can simply read about. You have to go out there and actually do it. As a final note, remember to keep a firm handshake. No one likes a dead fish.

Campus Dining

Although most incoming freshman may not have ranked 'quality of campus food' high on their list of criterion for the perfect school, this aspect of your undergraduate experience cannot be overstated. Here are some completely arbitrary numbers. The average student eats approximately 3 meals daily in addition to 3-5 snacks/late-night munchies. Assuming a freshman eats ~90% of his or her meals on campus, that amounts to well over 1000 food purchases on campus ! Okay, so those numbers really don't mean much, but you get the point: campus food is going to be a big part of your life. The following section will help you gain a general knowledge about campus dining.

PUBLIC WATER ANNOUNCEMENT: Wash. U. sells NO BOTTLED WATER ON CAMPUS. If you don't already own a water bottle, get one.

Meal Plans Tip: ORDER THE SMALLEST PLAN

Every eatery on campus accepts both meal plan points as well as campus card points. When you purchase a meal plan, each 'point' actually costs you slightly more than its value in dollars, and can only be used for purchasing food; campus card points are each worth exactly $1, and are used for vending and bookstore purchases as well as food (if you run out of points on your meal plan). What this means is that it always makes more sense, economically, to BUY THE SMALLEST PLAN AND THEN PURCHASE ADDITIONAL CAMPUS CARD POINTS, NOT MEAL PLAN POINTS !

Establish a 'Lunch Crew' for various days

Although there will undoubtedly be times during your Wash. U. career (midterms, finals) where you'll need to take a 'working lunch,' you should make an effort to be social and take a break during lunch. As many of your friends will have different academic schedules, it's important to take some time to take some time to coordinate lunches/coffee breaks with people. Whether you and your suitemates get a carvery wrap at Holmes every Tuesday or sit outside on the Ibby's patio Friday afternoons, it's refreshing to have a lunchtime social routine that helps alleviate the inevitable stresses of a fairly rigorous academic life.

Living

Breakfast
Monday thru Friday, the best options for a hearty breakfast are the New Bears Den and Einstein's Bagels (located in the B-School). Besides bagels, yogurt and pre-made breakfast sandwiches (which aren't that bad) you will struggle to find anything hearty for breakfast on main campus or the Village. Brunch on the weekends affords two fabulous options: à la carte in the village and all-you-can-eat in Bear's Den.

Vending
Although vending machines are located all over campus, those in the Law school buildings (Anheiser-Busch and Siegel Halls) provide a large array of food as well as beverage options. You can find hot-pockets and other meal-replacement type snacks at these locations in addition to the typical assortment of bagged chips, pretzels and candies.

DINING LOCATIONS

South 40

The New Bear's Den
Enter the eatery on the South 40 and you may believe you have just stepped into a exotic resort. Housed on the first floor of the residential college, South 40 House (commonly referred to as SoFoHo), this world-class college cafeteria and dining hall is central to all freshman and sophomore dorms. The new Bear's Den, which opened in Fall 2010, offers students a beautiful space to eat, socialize, and finish homework. The entire complex contains an assortment of individual stations along with Paws & Go market and Cherry Tree Café and Deli, all of which provide varied, fresh options. Once you get over their slightly clever, slightly insipid names, you can appreciate the quality and quantity of selections that Bear's Den provides. Below is a brief description of each:

Paws & Go: salad bar, fruit, ice cream, self-serve frozen yogurt, snacks, cereal, soup
Cherry Tree Café and Deli: coffee, tea, baked goods, fruit, custom sandwiches, soup
Sizzle & Stir: made-to-order stir-fry
Ciao Down: wood-fired pizza
L'Chaim: home-made Kosher selections
WUrld Fusion: Indian and comfort food

Grizzly Grill: custom sandwiches, burgers, falafel, souvlaki, fries, general grill food
¡OSO Good!: Mexican entrees

Tables and booths inside and outside typically guarantee enough seating at all times of day. Mod, colorful patterns line the floor and booths in the eating area, and the atmosphere is comfortable and cozy. The space even contains a fireplace and armchairs.

Around dinner time, student groups advertise at tables around Bear's Den by distributing free candy, selling t-shirts, blasting music, signing students up for events, or campaigning for leadership positions, all of which contribute to a lively, energetic atmosphere. Another busy time is 11:00 AM – 2:00 p.m. on Saturdays and Sundays when Bear's Den offers an all-you-care-to-eat brunch. If you attempt to sneak any food out, or share your food with someone who did not pay for his or her own brunch, beware: B&D security guards heavily monitor brunch activities and will chastise all naughty students. Aside from these formidable authority figures, Bear's Den workers are known to be friendly and sociable and are often on a first-name basis with students. Bear's Den's long hours make it a social scene until 3:00 AM, when the cash register closes on Friday and Saturday nights. There's no better end to a night than sitting with friends and rehashing the details of a good party while gnawing on an entire turkey leg, cutting into a gourmet lamb chop, or enjoying the popular "half-and-half" – a box filled with half chicken tenders, half fries.

Ursa's

Ursa's is located under Lien and serves wraps, quesadillas, smoothies, ice cream, desert and coffee from 6 p.m. until around 1am. I highly recommend the smoothies, ice cream and coffees, but would suggest hesitancy when requesting the wraps as the meat and rice tend to be dry if you order late in the evening (after 8 or so).

Paws&Go: The store formerly known as Bear's Mart

This is the campus grocery store, where you can buy most snacks or small food items you may need. BE WARNED: EVERYTHING IS EXTREMELY OVER PRICED. I would highly recommend purchasing food at Schnucks, the local supermarket located just south of the 40 on Clayton road (campus shuttles will take you there, but it is only ~10 minute walk).

Main Campus

Holmes Lounge (Connected to EADS, Between Ridgley Hall and the Quad)

Holmes lounge was originally built in 1904 for the World's Fair, a history that is certainly noticeable in the high, enchanting ceilings, rich woodwork and eloquent ambiance. Complete with a fireplace and various pods of comfy chairs interspersed throughout a sea of wooden dining tables, Holmes is a great place to enjoy a cozy meal with friends. In terms of food, the Holmes carvery offers delicious made-to-order sandwiches. Carvery meats are shaved for each sandwich, and the selection changes daily. Some notables include BBQ flank steak, rosemary lamb, and Carribean jerk turkey. Lines can tend to be long if you show up during rush hours (see chart), so my advice would be to grab a table and wait until the quarter hour to go get your food. Most importantly, no matter what you put on your sandwich, it always goes best with Rob's Special House Sauce, or if you can handle the heat, just ask Arthur for the "House on Fire" (house sauce + fire sauce, he'll know what you're talking about).

Danforth University Center (The DUC)

The ultimate main-campus dining location, the eateries in the DUC provide cafeteria style eating. Although every student will simply refer to this cafeteria as 'The DUC', there are technically four stations: 1853 Diner, Delicioso, Trattoria Verde, and Wash. U. Wok. Since these names mean nothing to any students eating in the DUC, I refuse to use them.

My advice when you first enter the DUC is to walk around to each station and see what makes you salivate most – I still do that every time I go here for lunch. The Asian station offers different dishes daily as well as fresh sushi; the vegetarian station tends to serve no meat; and the salad bar has a plethora of ingredients to choose from. The Mexican station serves a great taco salad and melts a mean quesadilla; when fresh, the sweet potato fries from the grill are great to munch. That being said, my strongest recommendation is the rotisserie chicken meal. For under $6, you can get a delicious piece of rotisserie chicken, vegetables and a starch. By far the best bang for your buck.

Café Bergson (aka DUC coffee shop)

This café offers smoothies as well as coffee and pastries. It is really cozy with large, plush couches and an extremely large flat screen television. The smoothies are a good option for a quick, light lunch as there are typically very small lines. You can grab a bagel or yogurt here for breakfast, as well as ooie-gooie butter cake (STL specialty) for a late-afternoon snack.

Ibby's (attached to the DUC)
Ibby's is Wash. U.'s 'upscale', sit down restaurant. Although many students tend to thing of Ibby's as a place to have a nice dinner on campus, it also has a fabulous lunch buffet during the week. For ~$10, students can gorge on dishes such as penne pasta salad with olives, sun dried tomatoes & grilled red onions, broccoli gratinee, honey-mustard glazed salmon, grilled chicken parmesan, and a variety of other delicious creations that rotate every day of the week. Many students also enjoy taking advantage of the fact that Ibby's serves wine and beer that can be paid for with meal points or campus card points. If you want to have a fabulous lunch, get a table on the Ibby's patio, hit up the lunch buffet and crack open a few bottles of wine. 96% of the time, you will get carded. Ibby's can get busy for dinner on the weekends, so if you plan on eating there with a large group (6 or more) you should definitely stop by or call and get a reservation.

Law School (Anheiser-Busch Hall)
Don't expect to use meal plan points here: the Law School cafeteria only accepts campus card points. That being said, this is a great spot for custom made pasta, stir-fry and fajitas, which rotate daily. You can also order custom deli sandwiches, grab a quick slice of pizza, and get your second-fourth coffee of the day. The atrium (located just in front of the cafeteria) is a nice place to sit and have a working lunch.

Stanley's (Formerly the Lopata hot-dog cart)
Located in Lopata (an engineering building on the east side of campus) this former hot-dog shack was known for its chili-cheese hot dogs served on Tuesday and Thursday. Now, Stanley's serves custom salads, sandwiches and wraps made to your liking, as well as the standard array of pre-made Bon Appetite affair

Subway
Subway is the last remaining franchised restaurant on campus (we used to have a Taco Bell!) If you get tired of the Bon Apetit offerings (which you probably will, even if you take my advice and get creative) you can always eat fresh. Although the 'rush hour' lines will look daunting at lunch and dinner, the employees are extremely hardworking, as well

Living

as friendly. Additionally, the relocation to the first floor of Mallinckrodt from rat cellar (area connected to the Gargoyle that the school will hopefully be turning into a student lounge/bar in the future!) has made the lines slightly more efficient. That being said, be prepared to order your sandwich when you are about 5 people away from the counter so that the line can keep moving. Even if it stretches all the way to the bookstore, you should have your sandwich in about 10 minutes.

Steinburg Café (Steinburg Hall aka Art/Architecture)
This past year the Steinburg Café evolved from a small snack shack to a larger snack shack: they now offer a selection of items that is identical to that found in Whispers.

Whispers (Main Campus Library)
Whispers is undoubtedly where caffeine addictions are born. Whispers offers a variety of pre-packaged meals ranging from fresh fruit and cheese to kosher salmon dinners. You can grab a bagel, coffee, and yogurt for breakfast, go to class, get another coffee and a scone for a snack, go to another class, return for an iced tea and an apple, go home and do fun things, then come back, grab another coffee, and get to work on your philosophy paper. Although the coffee sometimes tastes a little burnt, the espresso is always delicious.

Village Café / Market
The Village contains some Wash. U. favorites, such as stir fry and weekend brunch. Although the main grill remains open throughout the day, the stir-fry, deli, and global stations are only open during peak lunch and dinner hours, 11-2 and 5-8, respectively. In terms of sandwiches, the turkey and brie is fabulous when grilled as a panini. There are a variety of options within the stir-fry station. Choose from steak, chicken, shrimp, scallops, and tofu and a variety of veggies, then add some garnishes such as cilantro and jalapeño. Mix and match some sauces, choose between noodles, brown or white rice, and voila: made-to-order stir-fry. In terms of the grill, a Philly sandwich grilled with buffalo sauce is always a winner.

The village brunch is a great weekend morning routine that stays open until 2 p.m., as most partying patrons don't leave their beds 'till well after noon. From custom omelets and egg sandwiches to Belgium waffles and pancakes, the Village brunch will certainly make your hangover more bearable. It's also a great way to procrastinate that inevitable Sunday-long study session...

The Market is the Village equivalent of Bear's Mart, except it typically shelves some higher-quality snacks. Once again, unless you absolutely can't get to a grocery store, don't regularly buy snacks here, THEY ARE OVERPRICED.

The school has plans to renovate (big surprise) the Village Café, including more burners, fryers, a Paws&Go style salad bar, and an outdoor grilling area. While I will in know way claim to be clairvoyant, I think I can safely assert that, once completed, the new Village Café will function similarly to the old Village Café, but look a lot like the New Bear's Den.

Living

Quick Guide to Dining Locations

Location	Rush Hours	Late Night?	Best?
Whispers	10 Minutes before/ after the start of any class, 11-3	Closes @ 12	Pretzel Stick (great snack)
Einsteins	12, 1, 2	No	Bagel, lox and shmear; great deserts
DUC	11-230	Closes @ 9	Carvery meal, Asian station
Holmes	11-2 on the hour and half-hour	Closes @ 10	Carvery wrap with Rob's house sauce
Stanley's	11-1	No	Used to be chili dogs, now 'Lopata tower'
Subway	11-2, 5-7	Closes @ 10	Sweet Onion Chicken Teryaki (questionably)
Ibby's	Dinner reservations	Closes @ 10	Lunch buffet, Pesto Gnocchi
Bears Den	5-8, 2-3 (weekends)	Closes @ 2am, 3am	Anything combining ingredients from at least 2 stations (i.e. fajita meat & pasta)
Ursa's	N/A	Closes @ 1:30am	Frozen-slab ice cream
Village	6-8	Closes @12	Stir Fry, global fare (daily special)

Quick Guide to Dining Locations

Worst?	Coffee?	Healthy Choices
Pre-packaged Snacks (rip off!)	Yes	Yogurt, fruit, tea
Bagel Thins (they aren't bagels!)	Yes (Best on campus)	Salads, soups
Pizza	Yes (in Bergson Café)	Salads, soup, vegetarian meal
Pre-made panini (only in comparison to the wraps)	Yes	Soup
Salads are better elsewhere	No	Salads, soups
Seafood Sensation (unquestionably)	No	Almost everything!
Polenta	No	Salad, Omelet
Alfredo Sauce	No	Probably
Chicken wrap (tends to be dry)	Yes	Soup
Soy Nuggets	Yes	Salad. Soup

How to Get a 4.0
...While being a *Pothead*

Veteran tokers, newbie tokers, proud tokers, closet tokers, and even you never-toked-before tokers: Congrats! You got into Wash. U.! That was the easy part. Now, you must figure out how you will balance your incessant desire to light up with your societal obligation to succeed. Which one will win? Fortunately for you, they both can. Following my few pieces of advice, you too can get the grades...and the ganj. You heard me right. Contrary to popular clichés, you can have your cake, and eat it too. The whole thing. With your hands.

You're probably thinking you're going to have to work hard. Don't worry Cheech – you don't have to. You need to **work smart**. In order to do this, you need to make some very important friends, like caffeine. Need 6 hours to write a paper? No problem – your speedy ally will conquer it in 3. (Note: it might be 1,000 words longer than expected). And now that you've finished with so much time to spare, you can sit back, roll yourself a fatty, and reward yourself for a job well done.

Nobel Prize winner John Nash once said, "Classes will dull your mind, destroy potential for authentic creativity." What I'm sure he meant was it's important to **figure out what classes you need to go to** and which ones you don't. Look over the syllabus for each of your classes to figure out the attendance and grading policy, and the importance of assigned readings. Once you've got this down, find yourself some fine nugs (I suggest any sativa), and trust me, you'll be feeling that authentic creativity in no time.

Join the B-school. Remember, it's all group work – so let your group do it. Try and be the "ideas" guy (or, more realistically, the "highdeas" guy). If that really isn't your scene, **choose a major that compliments** your habitual use. I suggest Psychology. Minimal thinking involved, so class will definitely be more enjoyable if you are high as a kite. You're not going to become a psychologist anyway, so you don't need to worry about remembering things post-graduation. For you heady and more ambitious stoners, Philosophy also might work. If you can actually smoke and get a 4.0, you're probably already a PNP major. Or a plant biologist.

So there it is: A brief guide to getting by, to getting high, and being sly. Now if you'll excuse me it's 4 o'clock, and I've got a big date with my girlfriend Mary Jane in 20 minutes. She loves me dearly, and I really don't want to be late.

How to be "Healthy"

Everyone has heard of the "freshman 15." While most people don't experience the 15, there may be the 2, or 5, or 8. Given the stress of college and the need for quick and easy eating, the tendency for students to gain some weight is not uncommon. The most important thing to remember when you move into a dorm is that this small shoebox room is your new home. Being at college is not a vacation. The decisions you make during meals or the decision to be active should be considered as a routine.

A major difference between high school and college is the class schedule. Classes no longer take up Monday-Friday from 8 am to 3 p.m.. You will have classes as early as 8 am or as late as 9 p.m.. You may have one class on Tuesdays and Thursdays and four classes on Monday, Wednesday, and Friday. Because of the irregularity of a schedule, it is easy to skip meals and to let work stack up. No matter the time taken up by classes, it's important to try and have three meals a day. Make sure not to forget breakfast, it's the most important meal of the day! Even if your morning starts at noon, it's a good idea to eat something when you wake up. One way to keep breakfast in your regimen is to plan exercise in the morning. Whether it be a quick trip to the gym or a half hour of yoga in your room, giving yourself time to wake up and prepare for your day is important.

The food options at Wash. U. are great. People will always complain that they are bored of the food or that they wish they could eat off campus more, but if you ever have the chance to compare the cafeteria options of a state school to our options, there is no comparison. When you first get to school you will be unable to imagine what kind of spoiled kid would say such a thing, but it will happen to you too, don't worry. On the South 40 you will find a salad station, sandwich station, Asian station, southwest station, grill station, and soda... station. Between all of these stations there is an opportunity to pick fresh vegetables, proteins and carbs that will satisfy. Vegetarians need not worry; all Asian stations throughout campus have filling vegetable or tofu options. There is vegetarian sushi, soy chicken at the burrito bar, tofu at the salad bar, and a vegetarian station offering hearty meals at all hours the dining area is open. Without taking personal responsibility to include variety in their diets, students often get stuck

Living

ordering a half and half (half order of chicken fingers, half order of fries) for dinner every night.

While the gyms at Wash. U. have some room for improvement, you can get a great workout in if you plan ahead. Freshman and sophomore girls on ellipticals and treadmills most often populate the gym on the South 40, a.k.a the "estrogym." The small number of machines often means short workouts and lots of waiting. Because schedules are varied, if you can find a time during the day that is not in the morning or evening from 5-8, you will be more likely to have a machine for your full workout. The AC's gym is used by the athletic teams of Wash. U. and can be intimidating. However, the gym is stocked with freeweights and machines that can be used for an extensive workout. While using these gyms, the pool, or the tennis courts during open hours is a great idea to stay active, daily activities are just as important. There is a shuttle that travels across campus delivering students from the South 40 to the art school or the Village; however these 10-15 minute walks are an important part of being an active person. Choosing to walk to class, especially when the weather is nice, is a simple way to avoid being a sedentary person- especially when so much time is spent studying or in class.

One of the greatest parts about Wash. U. is that it is located right across the street from the Forest Park, the largest city park in the country. This beautiful gem is home to a Zoo, Art Museum, Paddle Boats, and History Museum among other attractions. There are designated paths throughout the park for walking, running, and biking. These paths measure anywhere from 2 to 8 miles and are a great way to spend time with friends or to explore what the park has to offer.

In addition to the many activities one can do in their own time, there are also classes offered by the school to encourage activity. The "estrogym" offers evening classes for Zumba dance or cardio kickboxing. These classes fill up daily and you can't guarantee you'll always find a spot. There are many courses offered by the school that are centered on physical development. Dance classes aren't limited to students in the major. The classes range from beginner's Ballet or Jazz to Couples Salsa dancing. There is a yoga class offered in the fall and spring as well as a year long Tai-Chi class that focus on a holistic approach to healthy living through the mind and body. You can also take weightlifting or independent fitness classes that encourage you to take the initiative to work out on your own. Additionally, there are a vast array of student groups that provide the opportunity to stay active, whether you enjoy playing ultimate frisbee or swing dancing.

Eating well and regular exercise shouldn't feel like a chore at Wash. U. There is always an opportunity for indulgence and college is certainly about having fun. If you decide to drink make sure you dance a proportional amount, or do pushups during your keg-stand instead of just holding yourself up. In order to stay healthy it is important to remember that this is your new home and not a vacation or "Real World St. Louis." Perhaps the most important key to staying healthy is getting enough sleep. College offers the temptation of socializing every night of the week. Choosing to be responsible and knowing there will always be another party another weekend is the best way to avoid getting sick or worn out, which will not only affect your health but also how you approach academics.

Wash. U.phamisms:

12) Mudd Field - p., Plays host to numerous IM sports throughout the year. Despite its name it is actually fairly dry given its placement in the open sun behind the DUC.
13) Francis Field- p., Outdoor turf athletic field. Site of the 1904 Olympics, making it a national landmark. This is also the reason we can't demolish it and build a real college stadium.

Living

The People You Will Meet
...On Your Freshman Floor

The Opposites: Every floor will have a roommate combo from hell. 8 out of 10 times it is two girls who would have avoided each other like the plague in high school. Your most classic roommate debauchery is the scholar versus the slut. One is hard working, doesn't drink, and is in bed by 11 on a Saturday night- just after she gets a little crazy and watches an episode of Three's Company. The other has seen the ceiling of a bedroom in every house on the row by the end of orientation. She can also be discovered by the receipt from her pap smear from the Habif Health and Wellness Center. It will take less than a week for these two to realize that their small enclave of property has become a virtual war zone. Sarah Palin and a moose would have made better roommates. Problems will begin to arise when the hard-working student wakes up to find a naked senior boy drinking her last vitamin water at 3 in the morning. The friendlier roommate will walk out of the bathroom, gargling mouthwash, and all hell will break lose. For the rest of the year the studious roommate will make her home by day in the library and take shelter at a friend's on weekend nights. She will only return to her room to change and shower. She tried to shower in the DUC but guess who she found making good use of the handicapped bar... Enjoy this clash of opposites while it lasts because once freshman year ends this kind of roommate disaster can only be found with the gem that is the transfer student.

The Suck Up: Without fail, there will be one worthless male soul on your freshman floor who worships the female RA like she is some rule-enforcing goddess who descended from the Heavens above Brookings Quad. Undoubtedly, this piece of work clung his lips to the ass hole of his overweight homeroom teacher in high school and is merely picking up where he left off. What is the attraction here? Her supreme knowledge of how to lead "Ice-Breaker games?" The way she always turns the television down exactly 12 notches when quiet hours start? Who knows. Either way, this kid will cling to her like she is the key to his academic and social future. She's neither. This unique example of a human being was shunned by his parents for a majority of his childhood and is seeking the approval of any authority figure he can find. He is the living embodiment of Dwight K. Schrute but has a much stronger prescription for his oversized glasses.

The Paparazzi: There will always be one girl on your floor who decides that it's necessary to have an obnoxious amount of Facebook albums featuring only people on your freshman floor. From the first album titled "My Freshman Flllooooorrr" (with enough repeated letters to give you a seizure) to the album named after that one inside joke you all share, "Who Leaves One Sandal in the Common Room? JK! LOLZ!" be prepared for a never ending stream of flash bolts and bullshit. So whether you are pre-gaming on a Friday or taking a dump on Tuesday everything you do will be photographed, posted, and tagged, by this excuse for a human being. Whoever bought this girl a camera for her high school graduation should be air dropped over North Korea. Unfortunately, you will suffer because she has decided to overcompensate for her lack of a social life in high school. The paparazzi killed Princess Diana and if you're epileptic, the flash bolts from this camera might kill you too. Save yourself the headache. Break her camera. You can take great pride in untagging yourself from every picture in the album "Last Alllbbuummm Before My Camera Broke :(."

The Pot Head: Don't look for the floor pot head at your first freshman floor meeting- he won't be there. He will be in his room getting high and staring at the four generic Grateful Dead posters he bought at the book store while wondering what kind of crumbs are in Trey Anastasio's beard. Your best chance to spot this red-eyed faux-hippie is on his way back from Bear's Den nose deep in a half and half while rocking sandals he got in middle school. He will then promptly return to his room where he pretends to be inspired by the excuse for an overdrawn music video known as Across the Universe. But ultimately, the pot head is your friend. He will always be there to make you feel better about yourself. When you sleep through your philosophy class, he'll sleep through two. When you don't understand your philosophy paper, he'll pretend to. And when you print out notes on that philosophy paper online, he will roll them up and smoke them. So enjoy the presence of this frisbee-throwing, festival-going, pseudo all-knowing 1970's wannabe's while you can. In time, the combination of drugs and philosophy will cause him to abandon school, work on a communal farm, and live in the attic of a poet/zen healer named Moon Cloud.

Your Roomate: "Everyone has a weird roommate. If you don't have a weird roommate, then you're the weird roommate." — Conan O'Brien

The First Kid to Throw-Up: Don't let this be you. You don't want to be the first kid to get way too drunk and hurl his St. Louis Bread Co. into the sink. But whether it's you, your suitemate, or the girl whose name you can't remember (Malinda maybe?) someone will be the first to boot and they will never live it down. History doesn't remember the team that finished in second so all vomitings after the first are inconsequential. Most likely, it will happen in the first week. Like BP in the Gulf Coast they will just let loose and contaminate every form of life in an immeasurable radius. The after affects will be unbearable. Statistically, someone on the floor will panic and call EST causing a routine yakking to turn into a crime scene. So how do you avoid this irreversible embarrassment? Two words: Dixie cups. A little known secret that will slowly permeate your freshman floor is that while Dixie cups are more readily available than shot glasses due to their inconspicuous appearance they actually hold more than twice as much liquid. This means that while your friend thought he was taking his usual 6-8 shots he is actually in the 12 to comatose range. When he ends the night (see 10:30) orally releasing his insides into the shower your fear of being the first to boot is over. Just make sure the paparazzi is aroun dto get it all on camera.

A Look at Wash. U.'s
Creative Community from Kuumba.TV

The creative community at Wash. U. is expansive. It's full of students performing, designing, creating, and collaborating. Just to list a few groups, WuSlam poetry performance squad, WuCypher Breakdance crew, RARA etc. This community exists because of the genuine curiosity to make an impact beyond academics. Most of our entertainment comes from the creative community on campus. In one week there might be an art show, a cappella concert, breakdance battle, and poetry slam.

Not only do we have all of these groups but they are some of the best at what they do. The poetry slam team placed 5th in the nation at the national competition last year. They host multiple poetry slams and open mics each semester, as well as weekly writing workshops.

On any given day at Wash. U. there is something creative happening. The events are accessible and well publicized. Then there are the creative individuals making t-shirts, posters, clothing, and music right in their dorm rooms. Every semester we have a festival, W.I.L.D., and in the weeks leading up to the festival, student artists will come up with their own designs and sell them to other students, publicizing their work and taking orders on facebook.

One interesting group is RARA(Residential Area Real Art), who create art galleries in various locations on campus. Students can submit to them with the chance to have their art hanging on campus for their friends to see.

An interesting thing about the creative community is that the power is in the students' hands. The administration doesn't create the groups or tell kids to start writing poetry or designing. Creative groups on campus are all student initiatives. They begin as ideas and grow into full-fledged organizations.

Kuumba.tv is a new project (and website) that started on campus this school year and documents the creative community on campus. The website offers video footage, photos, and updates about all the creative happenings at Wash. U. A part of the reason we created Kuumba.tv was to show that the creative community exists and provide further motivation for students to keep creating. We thought that if there is so much creativity out there at Wash. U., why not give recognition to those students and make sure they all know each other. With creativity being such a large part of our everyday experience at Wash. U., it now has a place to be shown and documented.

87

Top 10 Places to go #2

#10: B-Stacks, Olin Library – The only people down here are way too engrossed in their analysis of the implications of Walden Pond on East Asian Politics to notice you creep in and out. It offers seclusion, privacy, and there is always a good chance of vacancy.

#9: A-Stacks, Olin Library – One less flight of stairs to take when duty (subliminal pun intended) calls.

#8: Any floor of LabSci – Industrial-powered ventilation systems ensure swift removal of noxious fumes.

#7: The DUC – Although you run the risk of your lunch crew noticing that you took a rather long time to 'get a refill,' the flushing system is environmentally friendly. More importantly, you may need immediate accessibility after consuming a brick sized burrito. Their new design makes you feel as if you are truly in the comfort of your own home, and the walls from floor to ceiling between every stall offer an extraordinary experience to one's self.

#6: Mallinkrot – If you can make it here from the DUC, you'll be granted a bit more privacy and seclusion from post-meal traffic. Also if you live in a traditional dorm and are predicting a stinky storm, do your floor a favor and stop here on the way home from campus. The downstairs isn't used as much as it once was, and the fact that the bathrooms there are not well known make it an ideal place to spend time by yourself if you want to truly get everything out of those 7 minutes between classes.

#5: Lee 1 – Let's see how many loyal readers are out there (sorry Lee 1).

#4: Any Fraternity House – Just kidding. You definitely want to poop somewhere else. If you must, make it quick and pretend you were puking as this will probably sound more attractive to someone at a party.

#3: Anywhere on Fontbonne's campus

#2: B school second floor -- The stall has its own sink and mirror. Enough said.

#1:Earth and Planetary Sciences – This is by far the nicest bathroom on campus. If you have the time, it is well worth the walk.

Teaching Assistants

In many ways college classes differ from high school ones. Loose or nonexistent attendance policies, emphasis on a small number of key tests or papers and large amounts of nightly reading are mostly new experiences for incoming freshmen. Teaching Assistants, or TAs are one of these elements.

There are two types of TAs, each of whom can be used to your advantage in different ways. The first kind is an undergraduate student who has likely taken the class before, received a good grade and is now earning credit or a meager wage to relive the experience. The second type is the graduate student. Grad students love school (and hate work) so much that they have decided to spend the 4-7 years after undergraduate studying, researching and writing.

The undergraduate TA is less common in Art Sci and more common in the Bschool. He or she is usually a junior or senior and a very good student but maybe not a good teacher. There is a good chance that he doesn't remember some details from the class and if you are looking to have material explained you are probably better off going to the professor's office hours or the graduate TAs. However, undergrad TAs are often very good for explaining professor's expectations. What exams will look like, what professors want to see when grading written work and what major topics to focus on can all be learned from your undergraduate TA.

The dream of the graduate TA is to be the smartest person in the world in whatever class you are taking. Once he is the smartest person in that (probably unimportant) field, he wants to tell as many people about it as possible. These TA's will then often devote as much time as needed to explain the material, their views on it and their expectations on what you should know. This is very important as TA's are usually the ones who will grade exams and papers. The strategy is to then discuss your paper topics and exams with TA's before you write them. Then when you write them you already know what the grader wants to see.

Being a TA is a great option if you want to have something on your resume that really sticks out. Most larger classes have one, two, or even three TAs at the undergraduate level, and if you are lucky you may be able to find a TA in smaller classes. Being a TA allows you the opportunity to get closer with a specific professor, delve deeper into a subject you may be interested in, and make strides within your GPA.

Living

As a TA you can earn credit as if you were taking a class, meaning you will receive a grade for your work, and it will have an effect on your grade point average. For the most part, this is simply a perk—it is difficult to receive a poor grade while being a TA unless you truly neglect your responsibilities. In the business school you may opt to be paid for your time instead of receiving school credit. While the time you spend in class won't have any affect on your credit load, you will leave with a few extra bucks in your bank account.

As for the workload, it really varies from class to class. In larger lectures, most of your time will be spent grading multiple choice tests or smaller homework assignments, though higher-level classes may require more work. On student who was a teaching assistant for a 300-level political science course not only had to attend every class but was also required to take notes during lectures and mark down attendance and any time a student participated. Moreover, even though he didn't have to grade 5-7 page exam papers, he did have to peer review any rough drafts that students submitted, which was pretty much everyone. In comparison, a 200-level class only required that he show up to class and grade short answer questions in homework and exams with a provided answer key.

In general if you have some free space in your schedule being a TA is a great option, mostly because of the relationship you will build with your professor. This will be someone you can look to in the future for a recommendation or guidance with future plans, and of course provides a nice little boost to that good 'ol GPA.

Entrepreneurship
From the Skandalaris Center

The Skandalaris center is the center for entrepreneurship on campus. The purpose of the center is to generate interest in entrepreneurship on campus and support the entrepreneurial endeavors of students.

Idea Bounce

A few times a semester the center will host an Idea Bounce.: a competition where local community members and students to pitch their ideas for a chance to win money. A large part of the program is to connect students to the community through ideas. and give both a chance to connect with each other and share their ideas.

Coffee with the Experts

Provides opportunities for startup social and commercial entrepreneurs to have a 10 minute private conversation (and a free cup of coffee) with panelists with various areas of expertise, including experienced entrepreneurs, investors and service providers.

Youthbridge Competition

Promotes the development of novel approaches to social problems to enhance the sustainability of mission-based organizations, moving these social ventures beyond dependence on philanthropy and government. Throughout the competition, participants receive feedback from a panel of social investors and judges who are experts in social entrepreneurship and innovation.

The Skandalaris Internship Program

Offers students a paid internship during the summer with local entrepreneurs.

The Hatchery

Students form teams around a commercial or social venture idea proposed by a student or community entrepreneur. The deliverables for the course include two presentations to a panel of judges and a complete business plan.

Living

Wash. U.
Student Groups

I wouldn't join any club that would have me as a member

-Groucho Marx

Congress

Of The South Forty

One of my friend's professors once told her, "It's every undergraduate's prerogative to take advantage of all the free food on a college campus." For the broke college student living on the South 40, there's much more to take advantage of than just free food. Students on the 40 have access to subsidized sports games, trips to the symphony, events on and off campus, and free concerts and lectures.

The programming body in charge of planning, executing, and funding these opportunities is the Congress of the South 40. With a nearly half-million dollar budget, an office across from Bear's Den, and the ability to grant funds to other student groups, CS40 is the largest, most influential student programming body on campus and a vital part of residential life. This past year, CS40 brought the band *Matt and Kim* to the South 40 during its annual spring concert, WUStock. CS40 selected Frank Abagnale, whose life inspired the movie, Catch Me if You Can, to speak in College Hall. The student group sold discounted tickets to Rams' and Cardinals' games and organized outings to a paintball venue, Skyzone, a Vampire Weekend Concert, and a Lord of the Rings Symphony at the local Fox Theater. In addition, CS40 holds an annual Fall Formal Dance and hosts Residential College Olympics, an all-day affair in which residents compete in events ranging from Scrabble to dodge ball to a 5K race.

For those interested in getting involved with the group, many positions are available. Five sophomores (Speaker of the South 40, Director of Public Relations, Director of Development, Director of Services, and Director of Finance) comprise the executive board. Nine Chairs (Culture, Social, Sports and Recreation, Competitions, Sustainability, Academic, Community Service, Swamp, Internal Operations) report to the executives and plan their own events. Computerized polls open to all residents on the South 40 install new executives each spring, and the executives select the chairs, who must apply and interview for their positions.

Each residential college elects its own President, Vice President, Treasurer, Director of Public Relations, Assembly Representatives, and College Council Representatives. The Residential College Director as well as two RA's participate in College Council meetings and help students plan their own events, all intended to enhance unity and spirit among residents.

93 **Student Groups**

Weekly meetings, called assemblies, are open to the public. These allow a forum for Assembly Representatives from each college council to share their own upcoming programs and hear from the Executives, Chairs, and special guest speakers about upcoming programs for the entire South 40.

And there's always free food at assembly...

ThurtenE

ThurtenE Junior Honorary is an organization made up of 13 of the strongest leaders in the junior class. It was formed in 1904 as a secret society of men chosen for their leadership, character, and participation in campus activities, so it is steeped in tradition. The Honorary became co-ed in 1991 as it remains today. In 1935, ThurtenE was asked to rescue the floundering student circus from the senior honorary Pralma. ThurtenE rose to the occasion, steadily improved the Carnival, and made it into the exciting celebration that it is today.

The most visible aspect of ThurtenE, besides the bright yellow jackets, is the ThurtenE Carnival. ThurtenE Carnival is the largest student run carnival in the United States. The Carnival brings together over 50 student organizations, students from the Wash. U. campus and members of the larger St. Louis community. Net proceeds from the Carnival are donated to a local children's charity each year.

Taking up the most room at the carnival are the greek life façades. Weeks before the event fraternities and sororities pair up and pool together all of their architecture majors to plan out massive buildings that will house a play they will collectively put on. Until the event the architecture majors, and a few members who care a bit too much about Thurtene, spend night after night, drinking coffee after coffee, building elaborate façades. While the end result is always very impressive, the play is not why frats and sororities care about Thurtene. On the last night of the carnival the paired off greeks have Post-Thurtene. A night of incestuous debauchery, frat guys and sorority girls get more drunk than almost any other night of the year, hook up with as many people as possible, and then write poems about it the next day.

Other fraternities take different routes. Sigma Chi's pie each other with chocolate pudding (not the fantasy one usually imagines) and ZBT's fry anything you want to have fried (deep fried chipwhich is incredible) are just two examples. Many campus groups also have stands at Thurtene including ethnic food stands and a giant game of Rock 'Em Sock 'Em Robots from EnCouncil.

In the end, Thurtene is a time for Wash. U. and the St. Louis community to come together and enjoy greasy food, see a play, and whirl around on a ride or two.

A Cappella

For many people here at Wash. U., as a result of a lackluster choral programs, and the unwillingness to major in the arts, a cappella is where people who loved to sing in high school come to keep the melody alive. Therefore, singers divide amongst various backgrounds: from choir boys/girls to drum majors, musical theatre buffs and church singers. Though it is rare for someone to have no background, some of the best singers at Wash. U. have brought their talent straight from the shower and many groups encourage the inexperienced to come to tryouts. For some schools in the Northeast, joining an a cappella group is a rigorous "rush" affair. Although some people in the Wash. U. community center their social lives around the a cappella community, the process at Wash. U. is a little different. In 2005 an "A Cappella Auditions Council" was created to manage the "rush" process and allow students to survey the different aspects of each group. While this is certainly something you should take advantage of, here's a little insider's heads up on what to expect from each group.

The Pikers
This all-male group prides itself on it's good humor, entertainment, history, and a great rendition of "Flashdance." They also happen to be Wash. U.'s oldest a cappella group. Named after Wash. U.'s original mascot, the Pikers traditionally have had the most fun on campus. Rumors usually float around about exactly how spiked their punch is on stage, or if they do have a good handle of Jack before they start their concert "Jammin' Toast" in the first few weeks of the Spring Semester. All that being said, in recent years they have lost and gained talented singers, and still do an outkastastic rendition of "Hey Ya."

The Greenleafs
The only all-female group at Wash. U., the Greenleafs (whose name is a tribute to the Wash. U. co-founder) share a similar history to the Pikers as they were the second a capella group on campus. As a result of their sound, girls who enjoy all-female ensembles typically audition solely for the Greenleafs. They usually recruit one or two power singer such as Doni Muransky, though are most renowned for their classy rendition of "Cowboy Take Me Away."

The Mosaic Whispers

The Whispers are the oldest co-ed a cappella group on campus. They rehearse seven hours a week and take their sound very seriously. Their annual show "Splash of Color" is not the best concert to pregame, unless you can hold back your rowdy side and sit still for at least two hours. They are usually selected for nationwide compilations of a cappella such as BOCA or the CARAs because of their excellent recording, and were selected (along with the Amateurs) for the new Ben Folds a cappella CD for their rendition of "Still Fighting It".

The Amateurs

Featured on the Ben Folds compilation CD for "the Luckiest," this co-ed group tends to be slightly more laid back during performances. The Amateurs usually have a few amazing soloists that make watching this group an unmatched experience. They also rehearse seven hours a week and showcase the results in their annual concert, "Goin' Pro."

After Dark

Another co-ed group on campus, After Dark also likes to compete in the ICCA competition and records more than most groups on campus. They also sang a few songs for the famous Biden-Palin VP debate in 2008. Their annual concert "A Light from the Darkness" parallels the relatively common theme on campus of making a short film for their concert in which they sing during breaks. Their songs are usually pop-heavy and their old-school jams are sick. Overall, After Dark's quality, charm and style works, like Colt 45, every time.

More Fools than Wise

MFTW is a student-run chamber choir. They blow the pants off of anything choral and have always had trouble recruiting guys as a result of the subdued social culture that typically surrounds classical music performances. That being said, these guys certainly know how to party with style and woo the ladies.

Deliverance

A co-ed a cappella group on campus that sings Christian music, Deliverance has most concerts in Ursa's Cafe on campus and has grown tremendously in the last few years.

Student Groups

The Aristocats
This all-Disney a cappella group is balls to the walls awesome if you miss your childhood, like most people. Can you feel the love tonight?

The Stereotypes
Founded in 2001 as an all-male group, the Stereotypes have begun taking the annual ICCA competition increasingly seriously. The group prides itself on the closeness of its members, sometimes joking that it is a sorority. They dance and sing to garner some of the boldest soloists on campus. They have a concert in the fall called "Mr. Stereotype" where singers compete for votes and laughs to be crowned king in an all-male beauty pageant.

Staam
The co-ed Jewish a cappella group on campus, Staam has an interesting fan base and has recently had trouble recruiting Jewish members. They sing for Hanukkah annually and have recently tried their hand a few times at the ICCA competition with great non-jewish arrangements of "The Chain" and "Fa Fa". Quite a few singers historically have sung for both Staam and other groups.

Sur Awaaz
Under the leadership of a Piker, Aditya Nath, this young group of Southeast Asian(Indian) singers shows a lot of promise for the future.

The Burning Kumquat

Nestled between the Alumni House and the Butterfly garden, hidden by an ivy-covered brick wall lies a Wash. U. secret: The Burning Kumquat. In 2007, several undergraduate students who shared concerns about the state of American agriculture, as well as the many food-related social justice issues in the city of St. Louis, came together to start a garden. Today, there are many more of us--farmigarchs, farmers, and friends--who come to the garden for weekend workdays and gather elsewhere for movie screenings, t-shirt printing, and potlucks. Throughout the year we like to grow produce such as eggplant, okra, tomatoes, carrots, potatoes, garlic, strawberries, various herbs, flowers, microgreens and several experimental plants such as stevia. We love teaching others in the Wash. U. and the greater St. Louis communities about nutrition, the importance of cooking, the community garden movement, good eating, and creative expression. We see the farm as a shared space for experimentation, collective learning, relaxation, and art. During the school year as well as the summer we sell our produce to a farmers' market in North St. Louis, where we accept EBT stamps, and to Bon Appetit, Wash. U.'s dining service. The rest, we eat! This summer we will also be hosting the second year of Camp Kumquat, a gardening camp to teach St. Louis middle school students about our values. No experience is necessary to join us at the farm; we are all learning and experimenting together.

Student Groups

College Republicans

The College Republicans are a core of students with the stature and enthusiasm to survive in the liberal beehive that is Washington University in St. Louis. Unlike our friends the Democrats, we actually have to work to get people to show up to our meetings, and we have to call Student Life to get them to quote us – unlike the blue guys, who get the phone calls automagically.

Every once in a while, we'll join together with those on the opposite side of the aisle to have joint discussions at Pizza & Politics, or present more accurate arguments in the semesterly Campus Crossfire with the College Democrats. Otherwise, we have ice cream socials and try to co-program with other conservative groups on campus, like the Young Americans for Liberty or the College Libertarians, to bring conservatives out of the Wash. U. conservative closet.

Despite our David-esque fight against the liberal Goliath, we conservatives have managed to do much in our time here in Wash. U., including bringing top figures like Alberto Gonzalez and Karl Rove to campus. In the future, we'll be supporting the next Republican primary winner in the 2012 Presidential elections.

College Democrats

The College Democrats. If you came to just our first meeting at the beginning of every year, you'd think we were the biggest student organization on campus. You'd be mistaken – like any Democratic entity in the United States, we have trouble getting people to show up, but still manage to be loud and impactful throughout the year with our core group. Like the larger Democratic party nationally, we tend to enlist youth more than others, being one of the few groups on campus to allow freshmen to join our executive board (and then we have them do things we don't want to do – like paint the Underpass).

We put on a lot of social events through the year, from monthly Pizza & Politics discussion roundtables to chat about the issues, to showing off Democrat candidates to the student body via our Meet & Greets. We'll often be seen debating the College Republicans a few times a year at one of our most popular traditions, Campus Crossfire, and if you're on Facebook, you'll often be able to join us in protesting something or another conservative via a Facebook group.

What've we done lately? A couple years back you could find us in orange jumpsuits protesting the presence of Bush-yes-man Alberto Gonzalez, or, more recently, successfully protesting the potential-$20k-but-thankfully-aborted appearance of baby-maker extraordinaire, Bristol Palin, to talk about things she knows absolutely nothing about (everything?).

What's in the future? We'll keep on trying to get the one or two Republicans on campus to do fun things like Campus Crossfire and bipartisan Pizza & Politics with us to discuss the issues, but we're also big on national elections and 2012 is coming up. We like Barack for that one.

Student Groups

Red Alert

Wash. U. has an incredibly strong athletics program, but because we're in Division III, our athletes don't always get as much love as they should. That's where Red Alert comes in. Red Alert is the student-only fan group for Wash. U. athletics. We have joined together to support our fellow classmates, roommates, friends, and community members in their athletic endeavors. Signing up is free- what can be better than that? You'll get a free t-shirt, and when you wear that shirt to sporting events that Red Alert is at, you'll get more free stuff! We give out a lot of pizza, as well as fun prizes like jerseys, rally towels, and thunder sticks. We also run halftime contests and organize free fan buses to national championships when our teams (frequently) make it. If you have any ounce of school spirit, you'll want to sign-up and get your Red Alert shirt right away- they go fast. You'll get the occasional email telling you about upcoming events, so go get some free stuff and have a good time while you're at it!

Mama's Potroast

Mama's Pot Roast is a student-run improvisational theatre troupe at Washington University in St. Louis. We specialize in short-form improv (think *Whose Line is it Anyway?*) and sketch comedy. We perform at various on-campus events including Discovery Weekend and a cappella concerts, in addition to hosting several shows throughout the year. Our biggest show is Knight o' Komedy, a two-hour sketch and improv bonanza that takes place at the end of each semester.

According to legend, Mama's Pot Roast began in 1993 when two friends were talking to each other:

"Is there an improv group on campus?"
"No, I don't think there is."
"Want to start one?"

And the troupe was born. The name "Mama's Pot Roast" answers the question "what is something everybody loves?" and has been with the group since its first performance in the spring of 1993. On November 7th, 2003, twenty-eight Mama's Pot Roast alumni and current members celebrated Mama's Pot Roast's 10th birthday by participating in a gigantic, improvtastic jamboree. The twentieth birthday celebration will take place (intuitively enough) in 2013.

Mama's Pot Roast alumni include film star Peter Sarsgaard (Jarhead, An Education, The Green Lantern) and Second City improvisers Brooke Bagnall and Matt Craig. If you would like to be a Mama's Pot Roast alumnus or alumna, we would love to see you at improv auditions, held at the beginning of each semester.

Student Groups

ASA

Many people (read: members of cultural groups) believe cultural groups and the activities they produce run this campus bubble. Yes, there are fraternities and sororities, community service groups, social issues organizations, etc., but on a campus where there are so many different cultural identities, the cultural groups are it. My group, the African Students Association, is in that "it-ness". ASA started in the fall of 2005 when a group of very concerned students realized that most people pretty much sucked at having any in-depth knowledge of the African continent and its peoples. Many people allow what National Geographic and the rest of the media show them to guide their understanding of a place that in reality is incredibly vast and rich, and whose peoples are unbelievably diverse. We thoroughly enjoy every opportunity to change the way this community thinks about Africa. In fact, our most popular t-shirt says AFRICA IS NOT A COUNTRY. Hopefully people get this by now.

While ASA began as a place to rally African identities and battle ignorance, we've expanded our own mindset and have become a place for anyone with an interest in Africa. Every year there are a few event series that are hallmarks of ASA. These events are Africa Night!, where ASA members cook traditional meals from countries all across Africa; our Roundtable series which delves into topics of interest on and of the continent (we've had African ambassadors as guests); and the African Film Festival (wait, you guys make movies in Africa? Umm, YES. They win awards too); and last, but not least: Africa Week!, our largest production during which we do anything under the sun that can educate, entertain, inspire and make others familiar with the real Africa.

I have affectionately called the African Students Association "the little group that does" because we are a student organization that is comparatively small in number, but big in impact. We create amazing programming and as a result have generated great relationships, not just within the Wash. U. community, but within the St. Louis community. Not to wax emotional or anything, but the best relationships we have in ASA are with each other; we are like a family. Our motto and logo which is represented by an Adinkra symbol, appears on everything we have and do. That symbol and creed is "Unity Through Diversity." I've decided that it is fitting.

KWUR 90.3 FM
St . Louis Underground Radio

Broadcasting 24/7/365 from the bunk of the Women's Building, KWUR 90.3FM is one of the oldest remaining completely student-run radio stations in the country. It was founded on July 4th, 1976, but has roots that go as far back as 1961 in the form of KFRH broadcasting on the 40. Just find the most out-there, hipster kid in Whispers and ask him to swipe you into the station, since, chances are he's a DJ there. You can find everything from the latest Diplo mixtape to a live 1969 recording of the Velvet Underground in the Wash. U. Athletic Complex (yes, really). They have over 20,000 vinyl records lining their walls and just as many CDs on their shelves, every one defaced with KWUR DJ reviews. Even more beautiful are the KWUR walls, which are covered in years of graffiti and autographs from such visitors as Howard Stern, Ron Jeremy, and the latest it-band. Legend has it that Kurt Cobain signed the wall, but no one has ever been able to find the evidence. The station is a must-see.

KWUR is free-format, which means that, with proper training, anyone (even non-students) can take over the airwaves for one- or two-hour blocks every week for whatever purpose they want, be it to play their favorite underground tunes or rant about their least favorite Wash. U. administrator. Though the station only broadcasts at 10 watts, which is barely enough power to reach Gregg dormitory, DJs can reach a worldwide audience through kwur.com.

KWUR also has a recording studio in the station and, since the summer of 2009, has often featured local and national touring bands in their live in-studio series called the Stack Sessions. The Stack Sessions are archived on KWUR's website and have gotten the attention of the Riverfront Times, music blogs, and WIRED Magazine. Through its late-1980s/early-'90s magazine SAMPLE, KWUR interviewed the Beastie Boys, Sonic Youth, and dozens of other now-mondo-famous bands. Now, the station uses the Stack Sessions to hype bands like Band of Skulls, Passion Pit, Matt & Kim, and others more obscure.

In mid-February, KWUR always hosts the annual week-long concert series, KWUR Week. KWUR Week has had Brother Ali, Of Montreal, Thee Oh Sees, and tons of other acts. The headliners usually come share PBRs with Wash. U. students at a massive afterparty, too.

Student Groups

StudLife

From the Editor-In-Chief

A History

  Student Life, the independent student newspaper of Washington University in St. Louis, was founded in 1878, making it one of the nation's oldest collegiate papers. The newspaper covers the everyday goings-on of the school and surrounding community, reporting newsworthy events, the performance of Wash. U.'s sports teams and other aspects of college life. The editorial staff is composed entirely of University students.

  In 1999, Student Life became independent of the University with the formation of Washington University Student Media Inc., a non-profit company comprised of Student Life alumni, professional journalists, journalism professors, University representatives and other community leaders. The board provides financial oversight of the newspaper, hires the editor in chief, and acts as an advisor to the student editorial staff. All content decisions are the responsibility of the student editorial staff, making Student Life a free press, reporting the news as it sees fit and voicing opinions that are wholly its own.

  Student Life has won numerous awards throughout its history, including the 2009 Pacemaker Award—the highest honor in college journalism and an award that is commonly referred to as the 'Pulitzer Prize of College Journalism.'

Making the Paper

  Student Life hits stands three times a week and students and members of the campus community pick it up to see the latest campus happenings (and play Sudoku). While students enjoy the content of the paper throughout the week, few people actually know what it takes to make the paper every Monday, Wednesday, and Friday.

  The paper has a staff of 130 dedicated students who put in many sleepless nights to deliver the news to the campus. Staff positions range from restaurant reviewer, to sex columnist, to news reporter, to designer, to video journalist, to managing editor, to editor in chief and more. Students put in anywhere from 2 hours a week to the editor-in-chief's position which requires about 50 hours per week.

  Newsworthy events happen around campus every minute of everyday. In one news cycle alone, one club may be organizing its largest event of the year and another may be bringing a national political figure to campus—all while the University announces a policy change that will affect the student body. Despite what seems to be an infinite well of story ideas, every Monday Wednesday and Friday the paper chooses a finite number of articles to run. Finding the appropriate balance of news stories and creating a thrice-weekly paper is the product of countless hours of writing, researching and designing on the part of the news staff. From the first time that the staff sits together to brainstorm story ideas at the start of the week to just past midnight on a print day when the editor in chief finalizes the day's copy, the Student Life news cycle involves a myriad of students. And, whether they spend hours in the office each day like the senior editors, write an article a week like most reporters, or are just interviewed in Brookings Quad for a few minutes, every person within the cycle helps to shape the way in which news is presented to the University community.

A Typical Production Day

As mentioned before, the typical production for a single issue starts more than a week before the issue even goes to print. But most of the adrenaline racing excitement occurs the day before the issue comes out during a typical production day.

At 2 p.m. all the reporters and section editors start coming into the office after class. They put the final touches on their articles or columns, edit stories, and write any last-minute breaking news stories. All final content is due by 6 p.m.

Between 5 p.m. to 7 p.m. the design team starts to file in. There is a designer for each of the five sections in addition to a daily design editor and design chief. The designers have free range of creativity and figure out where to place the photos, headlines, and the rest of the visual elements.

Once the designers finish their sections around 8 p.m. they send it off to copy editors who are the last line of defense against errors. The better they do their job, the less you even notice their positions exist.

And finally the editor in chief and associate editor give the paper one final look through, PDF it, and ship it off to Louisiana, Missouri where the paper is printed.

But since we live in 2010, the paper is still not done once it goes to the printer. Next the online editor—with help from the editor in chief and associate editor—put the components of the paper online at studlife.com and prepare an email edition to be sent out to all subscribers.

Everyone in the Studlife family is fast asleep by 4 a.m. Of course like

Student Groups

all newsrooms, everyone meets deadline and everything goes according to schedule.

A Unique Perspective

Being a part of Student Life truly offers a unique perspective into campus life. As a former news reporter and news editor and current editor in chief, I have attended events and met people that I would never have been exposed to had I not been a member of the newspaper staff. I've had a 45-minute interview with porn star Ron Jeremy, brushed shoulders with top journalists and powerful politicians in spin ally at the Vice-Presidential debate, and even sat down and interviewed Citigroup CEO Vikram Pandit.

And that's just the famous people. Wash. U. is home to some of the most incredible, passionate and engaged student leaders. During the 2009-2010 academic year, activism on campus has been at its highest. From fighting for LGBTQ rights, to protesting the University's environmental policies, to supporting peer's in their fight against racial discrimination, Wash. U. students have not fallen into the trap of college apathy. Having the opportunity to report and interact with these students and see the impact that their voices have, has truly challenged the way that I think about the issues that surround me. Being a reporter and editor have allowed me to be in the middle of some of the most exciting campus events around the country.

As an independent newspaper, Student Life is able to challenge the administration and University policies when necessary. And while these headline events and investigative scoops do not happen everyday, each day is equally exciting as the student body and Student Life staff members continue to impress me with their innovative ideas and solutions to issues on campus. Not to sound overly trite, but being a member of the Student Life staff really demonstrates the power and scope of the student voice, both from inside and outside the newsroom.

Uncle Joe's Peer Counseling
General Information

Worst Case Scenarios

If you or a friend are dealing with anything that you feel is too big to handle, that you need someone to talk to, or that you need resources and help with, you can always contact Uncle Joe's Peer Counseling by pager at 314-935-5099 or at our office from 10 p.m.-1 a.m. in the Gregg basement. Also, Student Health Services is available for counseling or just talking with professionals – appointments can be made by calling 314-935-6666 or on their website.

Mental Health – Depression, Anxiety, and Other

Student Health Services

SHS offers a range of counseling and medical help for all students facing any and all issues. All services are confidential, and appointments can be madeMonday – Friday. Students have the ability to request their own counselors based on online biographies. The first 9 sessions are free and students are guaranteed 16 total sessions.

Health Promotion Services

Health Promotion Services provide information and services on issues and topics affecting all areas of student academics and health. All resources are free and focus on stress, anxiety, alcohol and addiction, GLBT, body image, relationships and sexual health, violence, and other mental health issues.

Student Health Advisory Committee

Student Health Advisory Committee (SHAC) serves a liaison between Student Health Services (SHS) and the Wash. U. student body. Through open forums and surveys, SHAC provides SHS with feedback directly from the students. In addition, SHAC works as a peer health education group by helping to organize De-Stress Fest, Sex Week, Safe Spring Break Week, and discussions for other health-related student groups. SHAC also makes condoms and information on safer sex available to on-campus residents through the "We've Got You Covered Campaign."

Eating Disorders

Reflections

Reflection is a student run group on campus that raises awareness about eating disorders on campus. Their programs include Love Your Body Week and Eating Disorder Awareness Week. Contact Reflections student group at Washureflections@yahoo.com.

McCallum Place
McCallum Place is an eating disorders treatment center in home-like setting. It has integrated medical and psychiatric care; providing psychotherapies and nutritional support for patients with anorexia, bulimia, binge eating disorders and compulsive exercise. Include residential stay, day treatment, intensive outpatient, transitional living, aftercare groups and support groups. There is a Support Group for people who are unable to attend a higher level of care that meets every 1st, 3rd and 4th Saturday of every month from 10:00-11:00 am in Clayton. There is a $10 charge for each session.

Sexual Assault and Rape

MORE
MORE is an all-male organization that offers an alternative perspective on how men can help prevent sexual assault and rape as well as ways to better support survivors. They present, write, advertise and speak out to raise public awareness about sexual assault and rape. They provide members with cutting-edge research, communication skills, and a chance to expand and shape their own and their peers' thoughts and beliefs about social issues.

CORE
CORE is a group of students dedicated to increasing awareness about the problems of rape, sexual assault, and intimate partner violence in the university population and the community at large, through facilitated discussions, presentations, and education campaigns. Every April, CORE brings Sexual Assault Awareness Week to Wash. U. with Take Back the Night, the Clothesline Project, and creative new programs, all in the hope of eventually ending the violence.

SARAH
SARAH is a 24-hour/7-day a week helpline that offers crisis counseling, resources, and referrals on rape, sexual assault, abuse, relationships, and

more. SARAH is completely student-run, anonymous, and confidential, and is open for access by any member of the Wash. U. community.

Wash. U.phamisms:

14) The Lot - p., The term for the parking lot in front of Brookings that plays host to the ThurtenE carnival. Full of fraternity pledges and sorority sistas, this will look like an unfinished construction site for a month, and somehow magically become a field of building façades during the 48 hours before the carnival opens. Don't mention "the lot" in front of any sororities before ThurtenE- you will likely be strangled.

15) The Loop - p., Just north of campus, the blocks of Delmar Blvd saturated with shops, restaurants and bars. Joe Edwards, a local entrepreneur, is responsible for turning the loop into one of the coolest streets in the country. Over the years he has built the Pagaent, Blueberry Hill (where Chuck Berry plays once a month), Pin Up Bowling Alley, Tivoli Theater, and most recently the Moonrise Hotel.

Student Groups

Wash. U.

Sports

We are in the business of kicking butt and
business is very, very good

-Charles Barkley

Women's Basketball

Bears basketball. It's like nothing else.

Lady Bear basketball has a strong tradition of excellence, lead by the fearless Coach Fahey, a woman who easily ranks as one of the most talented coaches in college basketball. Last year we won the program's fifth National Championship with a thrilling victory over Hope College in front of a crowd of dedicated fans that made the trip on a school-sponsored fan bus. Each game our enthusiastic fan base consisting of both students and community members show their unyielding support, regardless of score. This is undoubtedly one of the biggest reasons we continue to be successful. Next year, keep an eye out for a group of ladies dedicated to representing our school the best we can. We are all excited to get back to the hardwood and start working toward yet another successful season.

Something we talk about within the team is playing "94 feet," the full length of the gym floor. That means we don't take shortcuts and we finish every drill, practice and conditioning session from beginning to end. Our team gives up our Fall, Thanksgiving, Winter and Spring breaks to be on campus working hard so we can play 94 feet every game. This upcoming season will be filled with a challenging and exciting schedule. We're playing some of our biggest rivals, including teams we beat deep into the bracket the past two years of tournament. Get ready for an exciting year filled all leading up to the dramatic NCAA tournament.

Sports

Men's Tennis

The tennis team is good, and they really care about Tennis. Not convinced? Then read what one Wash. U. tennis player had to say about his team.

Three years ago, the men's tennis team won our first national championships in a close match against our archrival, Emory University. It was an experience that will never, and could never, be forgotten. Our #1 doubles team, Hoeland and Cutler, was down 0-4 and came back to win it 8-4 to give us the lead in doubles points and the final two matches left on the court both went into the third sets. Ever since then, our team has carried itself with the utmost confidence and has been regarded in the division as the team to beat. We've walked into each match believing that we have the skills to overcome every opponent. And though we were disappointed with our fourth place finish last year at nationals, we have since taken home our first conference title.

When I think about the players on the tennis team, I think of both athletic and academic excellence. I have never encountered a group of athletes so committed to their sport, and this talent and dedication certainly extends to their off court endevours. It is truly amazing that a team comprised of members from all walks of life, living completely different lifestyles can come together and motivate each other daily to compete for a common goal.

This year, we have acquired a few new incredible freshmen to replace our graduated seniors. We are one of the favorites to take home the national title, and while we may lack somewhat in experience, we sure make up for it with talent, dedication, and hard work. Keep an eye out in 2011 and 2012 for what is surely going to be an electrifying season.

Football

Playing for the love of the game.

Many people use this phrase in a cliché way or to describe some of our sports stars of America, but it probably fits best with Wash. U. football. This is why we play. On this level of football, attention and attendance at games can be sporadic to say the least. You won't see us on TV and you probably won't see groupies at games (we're working on changing that). Not to mention our facilities are less than flattering, which the school hides by talking about how "historic" they are. However, if you come out to a Wash. U. football game you will find a unit of student athletes that love this sport more than any team you've seen before.

In 2007, our football program capped a streak of 15 consecutive winning seasons. Yet, our program was somewhat overshadowed by the National Championships our other athletic programs tend to win. This past year we took a huge step forward, pulling off a 7-3 season and upsetting nationally ranked Wabash and Case Western during a 6 game winning streak. The passion our players have for the game definitely showed in our play, as we boasted several All-Conference and All-Region players and one All-American. Barely missing the playoffs last year after a close loss to Chicago (they lose at life though...) has been huge motivation as the team prepares for next year. We are returning a lot of talent on the defensive side of the ball and have an unbelievably deep receiving core that should make for an exciting 2011 season and maybe the best in decades.

Our team is full of outstanding students and players but more importantly outstanding people. Just like any football team, we can be rambunctious and have a decent number of meatheads, but it's amazing what we accomplish off the field when we have to get out of that mindset. The growth players experience on this team has revealed so much about life and the game. Come out to some games this fall, and see what Wash. U. football is all about. We're all-in this year.

Men's Soccer

The guys who play Fifa in real life.

Wash. U.'s men's soccer team has had an up-and-down past few years. They have narrowly missed out on making the NCAA tournament during their last two seasons, but three years ago made the Elite Eight (which was hosted at Wash. U.) and the year before that lost in the first round of the tournament. Hopes are high for this upcoming campaign, as the team returns eight starters and has a highly touted incoming freshman class. The biggest question mark for the Bears is at the goalkeeper position, as their previous keeper, four-year starter and all-region honoree John Smelcer just graduated. However, there is a very talented group of replacements vying to take his place. Look for the team's offense to come out blazing this year, as the attacking players are very talented and hungry for goals.

The fan support at games has been growing every year. Anchored by a core group of die-hard hooligans, things tend to get rowdy in the stands, especially at night games. Fans often paint up in the team's red and white or don various costumes. This leads to a fun atmosphere in the crowd, though things can get tense when the Bears are locked in a close match with a rival (mostly fellow UAA teams like Chicago or Emory). Though alcohol isn't allowed in the stands, fan pregames usually take care of that issue. Post-games aren't too bad either, as the soccer team is known for throwing some solid ragers at their off campus apartments.

Baseball

Showing off the diversity of America's pastime.

The baseball team is an eclectic group of guys from all parts of the country. With differing interests, majors, and levels of social skill, the love of baseball brings these guys together. The athletic department recently hired a new coach who shares a passion and love for the game. The youth and enthusiasm of the coaching staff is contagious and is sure to build a program that will be one of the best in the nation. Off the field the baseball players find themselves in different social circles; some in fraternities, others honoraries, others on the football team, other simply dedicated to the American pastime and their studies. Even though we are a Division-III team, many of the athletes could have competed at a higher level and the team is nationally competitive, frequently receiving a bid to the NCAA tournament. The team has training going on all year long, but is obviously more of a time commitment in the spring than in the fall.

Sports

Wash. U.phamisms:

16) Fist full of 5's - c;.,935-5555 is the number for EST, the student emergency service. Students will commonly refer to their drunken friends needing a "fist full of 5's" if they are face down in a bush with vomit trickling down their chin. Or if they fall off the clocktower.

V

The Lou

If you send a damned fool to St. Louis, and you don't tell them he's a damned fool, they'll never find out.

-Mark Twain

This Bud's for You

Whaaaaazup? If you want to have a good time in St. Louis, look no further than purchasing a case of Bud Light. But if that beer isn't fresh enough for you (the "born on" date is printed on the bottom of each can), take a trip over to the Anheuser-Busch brewery on 12th & Lynch Streets, less than 15 minutes from campus. A tour guide will take you through the factory, showing you the life cycle of the Budweiser beer that our country loves so much. Proudly displayed on your way in are the famous Clydsdales (the horses that you see in their commercials) "known for their size, strength, and precision" and if you're lucky you can catch a glimpse of that dalmatian too.

The tour is informative and you'll have the chance to see thousands of beer cans filled every minute, which is quite an inspiring sight. If you are 21, you will be treated to a tasting of the various types of beer that Anheuser has to offer. And if you are a criminal mastermind, you can craft a plan to steal the 500,000 cans stored in their massive full-warehouse refrigerator, which is fully stocked 365 days a year. Although native St. Louisians, along with many other Americans, have some issues with the company due to their sale to Belgian brewer Inbev, there is no denying that a fresh can of Budweiser tastes just as American as always.

Editor's Note: Don't make the mistake of ordering any other domestic light beer at a bar. You will be ostracized, criticized, chastised, jazzercized, vandalized and taekwandoized. You will also not be hooking up with anyone. So crack open a cold Bud Light, Mr. thirsty Wash. U. student, because this Bud's for you.

The Scoop on the Loop

When Bon Apetit begins to ruin your apetite you will need to begin frequenting the loop in attempts to appease your tastebuds. The loop has a plethora of cuisine types and dining experiences, as well as hookah bars, head shops, apparel stores, and of course, bars. Market Pubhouse is a promising new venue offering cheap(er) food and discounted drinks. There are rumors this new joint will stay open late and offer food--an option not available as of now. Three Kings is the local favorite when it comes to drinking. Its nightly live music, extraordinary beer selection, and proximity to campus makes it a fantastic option during the week if you want to grab a drink with a few pals. Blueberry Hill is another great bar spot. Great bar foods makes Blue Hill a place you can go early and stay late. Their dart boards and the expansive size make it a truly happening place. Most of the fun stems from simply exploring this social paradise for yourself; however there are a few things to take not of you venture out into the wild wild west.

Be weary of the infamous "loop characters." Many schemers and

St. Louis

panhandlers seem to be perpetually present on the sidewalk - don't let them fool you. Feel free to buy things if someone is selling them on the street (unless they are illegal substances, we don't condone that of course) but don't give a lady $20 to help her get a cab fair back to East Saint Louis. (Seriously, I've had the same woman tell me 4 different elaborate stories over a period of weeks, all requiring exactly $20. I don't mean to insinuate, but don't succumb to these schemes).

In contrast to their sleazy scheming counterparts, there are also some more eclectic and entertaining characters roaming the boulevard. One loop character, Mike, can be distinguished from the crowd by his profusely pierced face, crazy hats, and overly friendly antics with strangers. While he may be intimidating, don't be frightened! Mike is honestly one of the coolest people on the loop, and he is always entertaining at 1 a.m. when you're staggering back from the Pageant or Riddles with a hot dog in hand. If you're lucky, he may let you in on the secret handshake: five open-palm slaps, a twist around the thumbs, a joint bird flap, followed by... I've said too much, you find out on your own.

In closing, explore the loop, make your own hot spots, be aware of scheemers but don't be intimidated by cooky strangers. And never venture too far north of Delmar alone.

Forest Park

Beginning at the gates of Wash. U. and expanding over 1,293 acres (500 acres larger than Central Park in New York), is Forest Park, one of the treasures of St. Louis. Within the park you will find the Zoo, Art Museum, History Museum, Science Center, Muny Opera, and numerous golf courses. On a sunny day you will find people scattered across the lovely art hill picnicking, frisbeeing, and just having a great time enjoying the weather. At the base of the hill in the pond you can rent a paddle boat and make your way around the man-made waterways of the park. A great place to bike or run at any point in the year, Forest Park has something for everyone. Visit this place as often as you can. As close as it is, most people do not take advantage of all Forest Park has to offer. A reprieve from the stresses of school, Forest Park is the perfect place to get away from it all and have some time to relax.

Zoo:
Created in 1904 during the World's Fair, the St. Louis Zoo is the only place in St. Louis were you will find puffins and penguins living in harmony. The zoo is home to black rhinos, great apes, elephants, mongeese, capybara, and many other fun animals. It is a great place for anyone who can no longer bear the constant sight of the squirrels and bunnies that infest our campus and is in need of something more exciting, like the mongeese.

Golf Course:
The golf course at Forest Park offers 27 fairly easy holes, and greens fees that are fairly reasonable. In no way do we promote scamming the golf course out of these fees, but it is relatively easy to "walk-on" for a few quick holes in the evening for a twilight round of beer golf.

Art Museum:
At the top of Art Hill sits the St. Louis Art Museum. Featuring works of Titian, Michaelangelo, Manet, Monet, Van Gough, Kadinsky, Picasso, and hundreds of other artists, this Museum is not to be missed. The Museum is also constantly playing host to traveling exhibits of world-class caliber.

Science Museum:
Cool science exhibits. You got in to Wash. U. You're a nerd. Go check it out.

Missouri History Museum: You now live in Missouri. You're a midwesterner. Go check it out.

EXPLORATION: As mentioned earlier, this park is huge. On a nice day, grab a few adventurous friends, some music, a ball, a Frisbee, some beverages, maybe picnic supplies, and journey out into the park. It can be extremely fun to find your own little nook in the woods that you will frequent for the rest of your Wash. U. career.

Botanical Gardens

The Missouri Botanical Garden was built in 1859, making it one of the oldest botanical institutions in the United States. Despite its age, the botanical garden has managed to stay with the times and is arguably the best place in St. Louis to spend a sunny afternoon whether you're interested in botany, photography, sculpture, or just strolling through the beautiful outdoors.

The assortment of flora in the garden is staggering. Here you can find more types of exotic and beautiful plants than you could possibly imagine. Each species is labeled; small plaques give the scientific and colloquial names, and some list medicinal uses as well. For those of you not interested in plant biology there is also plenty for you.

The garden is maintained incredibly well so photographers, imagine the most pristine setting to snap some flower shots. There are no dead plants, no trash cans, and no litter to ruin your shots. Prepare to take some of the most stunning pictures of your amateur-flower-photographing-career.

For those of you interested in art, the botanical garden often features famous sculptors. In 2006 Dale Chihuly dispersed his glass pieces throughout the garden. The brightly colored glass together with the exotic flowers was absolutely fantastic. In 2008 Niki de Saint Phalle, a famous French sculptor, placed a number of sculptures throughout the garden. Keep an eye out for the next featured sculptor; they're sure to be awesome they meet the standards set by their predecessors.

Not interested in anything I've said so far? The botanical garden is also great place to just chill with your friends. There are a number of seating areas around the garden, some with benches, others with fountains; all are quiet, clean, and beautiful. It's not hard to find a secluded place where you can have some privacy. There are a few rules such as no drinking, smoking, music, or full-on picnics but the garden is expansive and security is sparse so you can really do whatever you want, as long as you respect the plants.

Admission is $4 for Wash. U. students, and free on Wednesdays and Saturdays before noon. It's a 15-minute drive from campus and parking is free. Make sure you get there at least once before you graduate, and I promise you will go back a second time.

St. Louis

The Confluence

Driving twenty minutes north of the loop, you will find yourself cruising alongside the magnificent Missouri River. Drive a little further and you will find the point where the Mississippi and Missouri rivers meet: The Confluence. The Confluence is in the national park, Columbia Bottoms, and is a hidden gem that most students at Wash. U. never even hear about. During the day, this beautiful location is a great place for relaxing, bird watching, or hiking. Marked trails will take you throughout the many acres of this unique nature reserve, up along the river and into the forests. If you are there between 5 and 8, depending on the time of the year, you will get a chance to see one of the most beautiful sunsets in the country. On a special platform, twenty feet above a field of wheat, you can slowly watch the night overtake the day, as the sun dips lower into the sky until it is forced beneath the skyline. Seeing this sunset with a few friends is a memory that will last a lifetime. And in January and February you can witness the amazing sight of migrating bald eagles swooping into the icy water to prey on the many fish that are caught in the frozen water. Have some faith, it's worth the drive.

Restaurants

Jimmy's on the Park
Classy night out location with wonderful dishes such as flash fried spinach which is a must. Half the restaurant is formal and the other half is not as formal (but still look nice and be ready for a $25-30 per person dinner that will leave you satisfied).
Neighborhood: Clayton 706 De Mun Ave Saint Louis, MO 63105
(314) 725-8585
www.jimmyscafe.com
Hours:
Mon. 5:30 p.m. - 10:00 p.m.
Tue-Thu. 11:30 a.m. - 10:00 p.m.
Fri-Sat. 11:30 a.m. - 10:30 p.m.
Sun. 10:00 a.m. - 2:00 p.m.
Sun. 5:00 p.m. - 9:00 p.m.

Khaldi Coffee
This is the coffee brewed at school. If you stop by their store (maybe a 7 minute walk from the 40) you'll find a quaint little coffee shop with a DELICIOUS variety of brews (you won't find this many at school) and some nice eats. It'll be a good point of reference for the cups you'll be poundin' back this year around finals time.
700 De Mun Ave
St Louis, MO 63105-2238
(314) 727-9955
kaldiscoffee.com

Crown Candy
One of the best spots in St. Louis (more based on the store than the location). In a slightly run down section of town this store serves up home made chocolate and other candy along with unsurpassed ice cream and a great selection of actual food too boot. Worth the trip for a meal (if you want to wait) or a scoop or a shake (chocolate banana will turn your life around).
Neighborhood: Old North Saint Louis 1401 Saint Louis Ave Saint Louis, MO 63106
(314) 621-9650
www.crowncandykitchen.net

St. Louis

Hours:
Mon-Thu. 10:30 a.m. - 8:00 p.m.
Fri-Sat. 10:30 a.m. - 10:00 p.m.
Sun. 11:00 a.m. - 6:00 p.m.

First Watch
The go to spot for brunch on Saturday and Sunday (when you're not at the village). They have an amazing selection of breakfast and lunch items. Lots of classics and some creative stuff too. The staff is as perky as the coffee (both are extra perky) and you'll be going there a lot over the years.
Neighborhood: Clayton? 8001 Forsyth Blvd
Saint Louis, MO 63105-1706
(314) 863-7330

Three Monkey's Bar
All you can eat brunch buffet done right. Creative menu items otherwise as well but on Sundays you get an omelet, pasta, and pizza station on top of an incredibly diverse tasty brunch buffet spread. ~$20 for brunch. A la cart food not on Sunday is cheaper.
Neighborhood: Tower Grove South 3153 Morganford Rd Saint Louis, MO 63116
(314) 772-9800
www.3monkeysstl.com

Booster's Café
This should be the hot spot for every Wash. U. student. Not only do they serve well priced delicious breakfast and lunch foods BUT it is run by a cute little group of older people that use the money to support their efforts to help those in need in Africa. Right on the way to the loop and worth the trip from on or off campus.
567 Melville Avenue Saint Louis, MO 63130
(314) 721-4499
www.boosterscafe.com/

Duff's
Wonderful brunch spot to go with the family. Always check on the specials. The biscuit and gravy special and banana walnut pancakes special will make your head spin with joy.
Neighborhood: Central West End 392 N. Euclid Avenue Saint Louis, MO 63108

(314) 361-0522
www.dineatduffs.com

Boathouse

Gorgeous views right on the lake in forest Park. Has patio right on the water which is perfect for brunch or lunch on a sunny day. You might hit a wait if it's nice out but it can be worth it. Foods good too. The paddle boats are actually really fun and can be a great workout if you go far enough. You can take them out to the epic fountains in the midst of forest park. Really fun afternoon and definitely worth the rental cost.
Neighborhood: Forest Park
6101 Government Dr
Forest Park
Saint Louis, MO 63110
(314) 367-2224
www.boathouseforestpark.com
Hours:
Mon-Thu. 11:00 a.m. - 9:00 p.m.
Fri-Sat. 11:00 a.m. - 10:00 p.m.
Sun. 9:00 a.m. - 10:00 p.m.

Rooster

Great brunch/lunch spot down into the city of STL. Nice flavor combinations.
Neighborhood: Downtown
1104 Locust St
St Louis, MO 63102
(314) 241-8118
www.roosterstl.com

Blues City Deli

Delicious sandwiches, lots of Po Bo's and other tasty cold and hot sandwiches in a part of town that is off the beaten trail. With free live fun Blues music on Thursdays (6-8 p.m.) and Saturdays (1-3 p.m.). Great sidewalk seating too if it's nice out and there isn't a band playing.
Neighborhood: Benton Park
2438 McNair
Saint Louis, MO 63118
(314) 773-8225
www.bluescitydeli.com/

St. Louis

Hours:
Mon-Wed. 11:00 a.m. - 4:00 p.m.
Thu. 11:00 a.m. - 8:00 p.m.
Fri-Sat. 11:00 a.m. - 4:00 p.m.

Adriana's

One of the best sandwiches in town. Highly recommend the Italian beef on cheesy garlic bread (it's called a Mary's Special and yea it is that good). Only open for lunch.
Neighborhood: The Hill
5101 Shaw Ave
Saint Louis, MO 63110
(314) 773-3833
Hours:
Mon-Sat. 10:30 a.m. - 3:00 p.m.

Companion

Tasty sandwiches and salads. Great light lunch.
Neighborhood: Central West End
4651 Maryland Ave
Saint Louis, MO 63108
(314) 352-4770
www.companionstl.com
Hours:
Mon-Sun. 6:00 a.m. - 9:00 p.m.

Taqueria El Bronco

Recently discovered Mexican restaurant. With a really funky atmosphere and very scrumptious meals. Only issue is that it's a little bit of a hike (it's near the airport and about 18 minutes away) but I believe it's worth the trip if you have a car and the time and a hankering for some good Mexican cuisine.
Neighborhood: Benton Park West
2812 Cherokee St
Saint Louis, MO 63118
(314) 762-0691

Schlafly Bottleworks

Tasty microbrewery beer and hefty servings of nachos...really hefty. If you like taking in the scents of hops then this is for you.
Neighborhood: Maplewood 7260 Southwest Ave Saint Louis, MO 63143

(314) 241-2337
www.schlafly.com/brewpubs.shtml
Hours:
Mon-Tue. 11:00 a.m. - 9:00 p.m.
Wed-Thu. 11:00 a.m. - 10:00 p.m.
Fri-Sat. 11:00 a.m. - 11:00 p.m.
Sun. 11:00 a.m. - 9:00 p.m.

Kampai Sushi
My favorite Japanese restaurant (just pushed past Nobu's on Olive which had incredibly fresh tasting fish at really good prices). I love the yellowtail and I'd recommend trying a fried sweet potatoe and avocado roll (sounds less than appetizing but is actually a delicious combo).
Neighborhood: Central West End
4909 W Pine Blvd
Saint Louis, MO 63108
(314) 367-2020

Eleven Eleven Mississippi
Delicious meal to go to with the fam. or a girl you wanna really impress. Great creative dishes but really pricey. Nice welcome to school restaurant.
Neighborhood: Lafayette Square
1111 Mississippi Ave
Saint Louis, MO 63104
(314) 241-9999
www.1111-m.com/

Joanie's Pizzaria
Thin crust, creative extra tasty pizza. They do something special to these pies and it's really worth it. In the area of town where the infamous annual Mardi Gras celebration is held in February.
Neighborhood: Soulard
2101 Menard St
Saint Louis, MO 63104.
www.joaniespizzeria.com
Hours:
Mon-Thu. 11:00 a.m. - 11:00 p.m.
Fri-Sat. 11:00 a.m. - 12:00 a.m.
Sun. 11:00 a.m. - 11:00 p.m.

St. Louis

Sweetie Pies at the Mangrove

Cafeteria style soul food. Some of the best fried chicken in town, amazing mac and cheese, great mashed potatoes and everything else southern. Spring for a combination sweet tea and lemonade (share it with other people..it's sweeeeeeet).
Neighborhood: Forest Park Southeast
4270 Manchester Rd
Saint Louis, MO 63110
(314) 371-0304

U-City Grill

Underrated staple of the loop's dining offerings. This restaurant has been open for 25 years and had to stop accepting credit cards because when it got busy it was inefficient to put through so many card. (NOTE THIS FACT, it's a nuisance to have to run around the corner for cash). The food is something most people haven't tried...Korean and it is a meal that I think everyone needs to try before leaving Wash. U. It is really fairly healthy and all types of delicious. I'd recommend the Bibim Bob (Rice topped with shredded, delicious vegetable and either beef or chicken [marinated to perfection], topped with a fried egg and hot sauce [note if you want less spice]. Also the fried rice is incredible but fairly similar.
Neighborhood: University City 6696 Enright Ave Saint Louis, MO 63130
(314) 721-3073

Protzel's Delicatessen

Another of my favorite sandwiches in Saint Louis. Great Jewish deli (not actually Kosher) that serves a sandwich called the John Carney (corn beef, pastrami, muenster [heated] and topped with cole slaw and honey mustard). My mouth waters thinking about it. Great motzah ball soup in the winter also. Perfect to cure any winter bug...
Neighborhood: Clayton 7608 Wydown Blvd Saint Louis, MO 63105
(314) 721-4445

Mom's Deli

Another wonderful deli spot where you gotta go with a Mom's Special and get ready for a big sandwich filled with deliciousness (I honestly don't remember what but it was good)
Neighborhood: Lindenwood Park 4412 Jamieson Ave Saint Louis, MO 63109
(314) 644-1198

O'Connell's Pub

Arguably the best burger in Saint Louis. Amazing home brewed pale ale and beer battered onion rings. Fries, grilled cheese (on a baguette that's flipped inside out...innovative) and Italian beef sandwich are all good also.

Neighborhood: Southwest Garden
4652 Shaw Ave
Saint Louis, MO 63110
(314) 773-6600

Pappy's Smokehouse

Super tasty smokey barbeque. Brisket, chicken and ribs are the specialties with great sauces. Over by SLU's campus a little. Tasty fun meal.

Neighborhood: Midtown
3106 Olive St
St Louis, MO 63103
(314) 535-4340
pappyssmokehouse.com
(314) 865-1994

St. Louis

VI

Wash. U.
Greek Life

Christ, seven years of college down the drain.

-John Belushi

Understanding This Section

The greek life section was created to give you a stereotypical idea of what each fraternity and sorority is like. However greek organizations, like many organizations, are careful to maintain a positive reputation on campus. While this fact is no doubt understandable, it proved to be an impediment to making this book. As we reached out to the greek community for article submissions, we faced resistance--a few fraternities ignored us and none of the sororities wanted to have an article written about them. The beauty of Bear It All is that you get to hear the voice of someone who is highly involved with the topics at hand, so the lack of involvement was disappointing. Because we believe that you deserve to know at least something about greek organizations, we have included articles anyway. Articles about fraternities that didn't respond are from the 2010-2011 version of Bear It All, while the sorority articles are all quotes from their chapter websites or national websites.

We hope that while this section will give you a little insight into each frat and sorority, you will still spend the time to get to know the greek organizations on a personal basis. These summaries are in no way complete, and the only way to figure out where you want to join is to get to know the brothers and sisters that make up the organization. No decisions should be based solely on our descriptions. In fact, no decisions should be based in any way on our descriptions. If you don't join a house based on the superficial information provided, then you are missing the whole point of first semester and the entire recruitment process. Don't make your rush decision based on stereotypes: go out and meet the members!

Every greek organization has their stereotypes, and we asked each organization to play off them. Some had more success than others, but we find the section to be humorous and semi-informative. As with everything else, this is just a guide.

Greek Life

Wash. U.

Rush

Fraternity Rush

You come back from winter break feeling refreshed and ready to jump back into life at Wash. U. The first week you spend your days running around finding your classes in buildings you've never been in before and your nights partying like it's 2099. Your feet and your liver will be begging for another vacation. Lucky for you, weeks two, three, and four bring fraternity rush, some of the best weeks of the semester.

But let's pause here and get something straight. Although formal rush takes place second semester, rushing takes place from the day you step on campus. The second you walk into a fraternity party, rush has begun, so make sure your beer pong skills and dance moves are flawless (just kidding, my only dance move is the sprinkler).

After the first week of second semester, rush will begin. What do you need to know? Rush is a period of official (and unofficial) events held by fraternities to spend time with potential "pledges." Until you join a fraternity you are a rush. As a rush you can expect lots of free food, lots of free trips, and lots of free booze. The first two weeks of rush are open, which means that you can attend the events of any fraternity. Open rush is followed by closed rush, in which frats invite certain rushees to events that are closed off to the rushing public, so that potential pledges and brothers can get to know each other even more. It is a good sign if you get an invitation to closed rush, but it's not the golden ticket.

When rush ends, you will most likely get a bid from the fraternity or fraternities that you have clicked with. A bid means that the fraternity is inviting you to become a member of the team. You will have two days to decide which frat you want to join, if you want to join at all. On the night of bid acceptance, you will show up to the fraternity of your choice, and experience the pledge initiation rituals of your fraternity. But you're not a member yet. When you accept your bid you become a pledge. You will be a pledge for a certain amount of time before you become a member. As the saying goes, "pledging is the most fun you'll never want to have again."

Now you must be wondering: how do I get a bid? The best advice I can give is not to try too hard. During first semester, nothing is more off-putting to a brother than a freshman who begins talking about joining a fraternity. You will probably have a lot of questions, but those should wait until you get closer to rush. First semester is a time to check out all of the different fraternities and get to know the brothers. As the semester goes by, you will find that certain houses appeal to you more than others, and you will begin to spend more time with the brothers from those houses. Try and meet as many brothers as possible. If you present yourself as an outgoing friendly guy, it can only help to know more people. Most important however is not to try and shake hands with as many brothers as possible but rather to try and really get to know them. It's better to be very friendly with one brother than it is to know the names of five. When brothers decide who they are giving bids to, they need to feel confident that they know who you are and how you fit into the culture of the fraternity.

In the end, don't put too much thought into the process - it should be fun, not stressful. Be friendly, outgoing, and most importantly, be yourself. These are the only ways to guarantee you make it into the right house and have a fulfilling Greek experience. Do not try and prove to brothers how much you can drink. Play pong with brothers, shotgun with brothers, have fun with brothers, but don't think that your drinking ability will impress brothers. Wash. U. has been cracking down on Greek Life over the past few years, and you don't want brothers to view you as a liability. So have fun, but don't think that your morning after story about how you woke up with a vomit covered blanket will get you a bid. Although if you had a girl with you, maybe it could...

Do's and Don'ts

Of fraternity rush

Do: Rush a fraternity. Even if you don't think frats are your thing, you might be surprised.

Don't: Talk about how you drank higher quality beer in high school. Natty is our God, and it will be yours too.

Do: Go out on Tuesdays and Wednesdays. They can often be the best nights of the week.

Don't: Ask a brother which fraternities are the best, or why one fraternity is better than another. Come to these conclusions yourself.

Do: Hang out with brothers in your down time. The best way to get to know a brother, and his house, is outside of the party setting, a fact that any brother can attest to.

Don't: Puke on a cop car after coming from a frat party.

Do: Have the courage to hang out at frats, even if your friends don't. You can join different fraternities than your friends while maintaining these friendships.

Don't: Hit on a brother's girl. Ever.

Do: Try out a bunch of fraternities. Just because you like the first one you come to doesn't mean it's the best for you.

Don't: Act too confident during rush. The last thing any brother wants to see is a freshman assuming he's in the fraternity before he even gets offered a bid.

Greek Life

Sorority Rush

If sorority life is something you'd like to explore while in college, then you'll have to endure the week-long speed dating that Wash. U.'s Greek Life Office likes to refer to as "recruitment." If you choose this route, then be prepared to return to school in the winter, a week before school actually starts. Wash. U. endorses delayed rush, which just means that they give freshman all of first semester to settle into dorm life, establish their own friends, and get involved in other on-campus activities before they are stormed with the prospect of meeting 700 new girls. While your friends at other schools are going through rush in the fall, you may think you can relax and delay all the judgment and fake conversation. But beware, sororities are already turning on their radars the first day of school. Way before sorority rush even begins, the actives recommend girls who they've met and think would be a good fit for their sorority. Actives in the sorority are on the lookout when they are in class and when they are out partying, so make an effort to meet older girls. Not only is this a good way to get your name out there, it also helps you filter through the stereotypes and decide for yourself which one is the best for you. Warning: they have eyes everywhere so watch out when you decide to dance on top of that table in the basement of a fraternity. You wouldn't want to get blacklisted for a night you don't even remember.

However, this shouldn't discourage your decision to join a sorority. At the risk of sounding cliché, the truth is that sororities provide an intimate community, and many friendships made in them are life long. While you may believe that you have a lot of friends after your first few months at Wash. U., the amount of friends you make after going through rush grows exponentially. Every older girl in the sorority wants to meet the product of their hard work during rush (the new members!), so get ready to be showered in gifts and girl dates galore. And of course, there will never be a month at Wash. U. without some sort of fun dress-up event planned. Each sorority plans so many drunken festivities that are just calling for you to bust a move on the dance floor.

The first step is to sign up so that the GLO recruitment chairs can put you in a recruitment group led by a Gamma Chi (a girl from one of the 7 sororities who has temporarily disaffiliated in order to give you an unbiased opinion). There are five days of formal recruitment and you get a break day in the middle. Each day, you will visit multiple sororities and meet a myriad of girls fraught with excitement to meet you and already knowing creepily too much information about you. At the end of each day, you'll meet with your Gamma Chi to discuss your opinions about each sorority and rank your top favorites. At Wash. U., we have Chi Omega, Delta Gamma, Kappa Kappa Gamma, Alpha Phi, Phi Beta Phi, Alpha Epsilon Phi, and Alpha Omega Pi. Each chapter has their own way of selecting new members, so remember to be genuine but also keep in mind that the selection process is mutual and they are taking mental notes just as intensely as you are. Under all this pressure, it's easy to break out in a sweaty stench which can be especially devastating in the close quarters of the rooms on campus. So apply enough deodorant under your stylish top to keep yourself (and everyone else) calm, cool, and collected.

The first day is "Go Greek." On this day, your Gamma Chi will take you and your recruitment group of about 10 other girls to visit each of the seven sororities. This day is fast paced and long! You'll be talking to about 5 girls from each sorority. The conversation today will cover the basics: dorm life, your hometown, your major, and other things you might talk to someone about when you first meet them. The conversations get pretty boring by the 7th party, so try to keep up your enthusiasm and keep the conversation lively. The actives will appreciate (and take note) of any sort of effort you make to spice up your chat. If conversation is truly lagging, that might be an indication that it's not the sorority for you. And to top it all off, you don't need to make any decisions after this horribly long day! Every girl gets to return to every chapter the next day, so be sure to rest up for round 2 of recruitment.

The second day is Philanthropy Day. This is when the sorority will introduce the philanthropy organization that they contribute to. On top of speaking with girls in the sorority, you will hear officers of the chapter discuss what they do and why it is important. At the end of this day, you'll select your top three choices with your Gamma Chi.

The third day is called Outsides. Not to be confused by the title, Outsides take place indoors and you'll get to see the sisters acting a little more sassy. This is a fun day where you'll be entertained by the chapter's showcase of their talents in songs and skits. You'll also have a bit more time to spend with each girl to help you refine your decision of your number one.

The fourth day is Preferences. This day is when the chapter shares a special ceremony with all the girls they have invited back.

141   **Greek Life**

You'll be able to return to a maximum of three sororities. On this day, the attire is dressy and the conversation more intimate. You will speak with one girl and by the end of the day, you will put your top and final choice as to who you want to be your future sisters. Don't be afraid to ask questions and find out what you really want to know from each sorority. The more you know about each one, the more it will help you to make a decision in the end..

The final day is Bid Day when you finally find out which sorority you will be spending your next four years with!

The entire week is a long and exhausting social rollercoaster. The cheering and singing might become overwhelming at times, but just remember to be genuine and you'll have the time of your life. Be prepared for the ups and downs, the awkward conversations, and the circulating stereotypes. On decision day, don't be scared about offending a girl if you decide not to choose her sorority. In the end, each girl had to go through the same decision, and it's merely a formality in the rush experience. And after it's all over, go ahead and say hello to a girl you met at a party or facebook a girl you really enjoyed chatting with. Expanding your social circle is a perk of rush, so run with it! When it comes down to it, choosing your sorority ought to be based on the girls who you could see yourself being the most comfortable with whenever and wherever—whether it's partying, chatting over coffee, or just watching movies in your dorm room.

Sorority Terms You Need to Know:

Active- a girl who is already a member in a sorority

Blacklisted- a status designating that a girl is banned from consideration in a sorority

Gamma Chi- a girl who has temporarily disaffililated from her sorority to act as an unbiased counselor to you during your rush experience

GLO- greek life office

PNM- potential new member

Wash. U.
Fraternities

Greek Life

Sigma Chi

A fan of this house might say: Since its foundation at Wash. U. in 1903, Sigma Chi brothers have been involved all across campus. We are proud of the fact that all of our brothers come from varying backgrounds and are all very different from each other. Our guys are involved everywhere, including varsity sports, numerous student groups, and philanthropic organizations. Brothers have become founders of organizations such as The Solution, Olin Sports Management Organization, Books and Basketball, and Koaches 4 Kids. We've got Danforth Scholars, business owners, marathon runners and the like. As a chapter, we have won the Peterson Award multiple times, the highest award given to any Sigma Chi chapter. As Charlie Sheen would put it, we're bi-winners. Though some say we are exclusive and not open to the wider campus, this belief is most likely born out of our brothers being as close as they are...bro's will be bro's. But don't be intimidated if you come across a group of us, and don't be turned off either if we seem to be happily caught up in one another. It's in the nature of being a bro, bro.

A hater of this house might say: They come off as very elitist and selective so if you're not friends with any of them don't bother trying to get into one of their parties; it probably won't be fun anyway if you don't know someone.

Most Likely seen wearing: Sigma Chi T-Shirt, Sigma Chi Sweatshirt, Sigma Chi Hat, Sigma Chi Sweatpants, Sigma Chi Glasses

Guys Rushing...
Often Consider: SigEp, Phi Delt
Sometimes Consider: Kappa Sig, SAE
Rarely Consider: TKE, Theta Xi

Sig Ep

A fan of this house might say: The house's over arching quality is its diversity—a characteristic represented in members' embracing the saying "keep Sig Ep weird." Indeed there is a strangeness that jocks, preps, hipsters, business owners, architects, and historians can coalesce into as close of a brotherhood as Sig Ep is. Members are leaders in activities in and out of greek life, some of which include a capella groups, student government, community service clubs, and varsity athletics. You're likely to see a group of Sig Eps getting fratty at any social event—from sorority formals to Art Prom—and chanting fraternity songs all the while. They participate in various community service activities including ThurtenE, where they develop bonds with Alpha Phi. Sig Eps succeed academically as well, continually holding one of the top GPAs of all Wash. U. fraternities. Amid their success, there is a thread of mischievousness in their house that is usually manifested in good-hearted jokes and pranks on one another. In the end, it is this openness and acceptance of each other's differences that has made Sig Ep the fun-loving and tight brotherhood it is.

A hater of this house might say: The scene of a sweaty basement with scores of drunk freshmen/Alpha Phi's making out with each other is a classic Sig Ep image and the ubiquity of these parties typically bores most party-goers after a few months into the year. Some members rank pretty high on the weirdness scale. They love to love each other, but they love their reflections even more.

Most likely seen wearing: Custom-fit Polos, Sig Ep lax pennies, and tight fitting Alpha Phi sweaters

Guys Rushing:
Often Consider: Sigma Chi, AEPi
Sometimes Consider: Phi Delt, Sammy
Rarely Consider: TKE, Beta,

Greek Life

AEPi

A fan of this house might say: Alpha Epsilon Pi has had another successful year initiating 18 new members and contributing to Wash. U.'s strong Greek community. They have a close brotherhood of guys with diverse interests. They have leaders in various groups including CPC, Team 31, Varsity Sports and the StEP program. They do surprisingly good academically and are very visible in the B-School. If you are looking to have a fun, chill night there is always someone in the house willing to join you. The house has one of the largest basements on campus and is utilized well, during events such as its annual Black Hole party. Definitely people who know how to have fun, but are down to earth as well.

A hater of this house might say: They can be too exclusive, and can be assholes at their door. Many come from the same standard northeast Jewish background. Not being on the upper row is a con. Weak philanthropy event. You are more likely to see these guys bbming in the B-school lounge than fratting it up on their patio.

Most likely seen wearing: Two Piece Suit and Bluetooth earpiece.

Guys Rushing...
Often consider: Sammy, SigEp
Sometimes Consider: SigNu, SAE
Rarely Consider: Phi Delt, Sigma Chi

Phi Delt

Though known for consisting primarily of current and former football players, Phi Delt is comprised of a pretty diverse mix of athletes including baseball players, soccer players, and the world's cupstacking champion from 2007 (not kidding).

A fan of this house might say: Fun, meaty, midwestern folk who love to party. Comprised mainly of athletes, the house is super competitive as both participators and spectators of sports. Specifically, Phi Delt was instrumental in creating some semblance of spirit at this school via The Bomb Squad, a roudy group of fans that can be seen at every home basketball game.

A hater of this house might say: Arrogant, asshole, meatheads (This is all true, but we take a lot of pride in this stereotype). They can be exclusive and get real aggressive when shit hammered.

Most Likely seen wearing: Camo Man Tank with Eye Black

Guys Rushing:
Often Consider: Kappa Sig, Sigma Chi
Sometimes Consider: Sammy, SigEp
Rarely Consider: Beta, TKE

Editor's Note: It's true. The bomb squad is the only driving force of school spirit at Wash. U. No matter how much the school tries, no one will ever care about Wash. U.sports. Without the bomb squad our "stadiums" would be empty. Thanks guys.

Greek Life

SAE

A fan of this house might say: The SAE chapter at Wash. U. is rather unique because of the fact that it was quite recently re-built. Since it's so small, new members have a pretty good chance of significan'tly impacting the future image and direction of the fraternity. There is no specific stereotype that describes SAE, largely because its old stereotypes were shattered in the re-building process when they lost their house. Those that contributed to giving it that stereotype were forced out of the frat. These days, the brotherhood is so diverse that minor conflicts—more funny than serious—arise constantly. For instance, the issue of whether it is okay to wear Nike Dunks and a 59-Fifty with a suit. Or whether Lynyrd Skynyrd or Animal Collective should be next on the playlist. In fact, you are likely to find equal numbers Creative Recreation's, Sperry's, and penny loafers in a group of SAE's. Members of these groups regard each other with either keen curiosity or utter bewilderment. In rough times we have kept our presence on campus through our annual philanthropy dodgeball tournament, Dodging Depression. The Chapter has spent the last few years working towards specific goals such as maintaining national recognition, re-attaining school recognition, and re-gaining a House on campus. All these completed, I believe the next year will be spent working towards a more rewarding objective: making sure you know who the fuck we are. Pardon me, whom.

A hater of this house might say: SAE is currently in the rebuilding stage. Whether they are building with straw or bricks is yet to be seen.

Most likely seen to be wearing: Creative Recreation's, Sperry's, or penny loafers

Guys Rushing...
Often Consider: Sigma Chi, Sammy, ZBT
Sometimes Consider: Kappa Sig, Sig Ep
Rarely Consider: Theta Xi, Beta

Kappa Sig

Beta

The Alpha Iota chapter of Beta Theta Pi, founded in 1869, was the first fraternity on Wash. U.'s campus. Beta is one of the largest chapters on campus, and following the Spring 2010 pledge class initiation will have over 80 active brothers.

A fan of this house might say: They're a great group of guys who are very involved around campus and known as "the nice guys your mom would want your sister to date." They have historically been the most represented fraternity among Wash. U. Student Associates and Residential Advisors, and are involved in a huge number of student groups around the school. While they don't have parties as often as some other houses, the parties that they do throw are very well attended and are well-known for being a great time for people who want to party as well as people who just want to dance.

A hater of this house might say: They are lame because they don't throw as many open parties as some other fraternities. If you attend their annual bubbles party, consider wearing a body sized condom. If you need a good night's sleep, this is the place to be.

Most likely seen wearing: Christmas sweater from grandma

Guys Rushing...
Often Consider: TKE, Theta Xi
Sometimes Consider: AEPi, SigNu
Rarely Consider: Phi Delt, SigEp

ZBT

A fan of this house might say: Good lord do these guys know how to have a good time. They manage to throw down pretty hard without all the legal troubles that the rest of the other fun fraternities have been dealing with. Despite the reputation of being a bunch of potheads, ZBT actually boasts one of the top GPAs in all of Greek Life, including a stable of pre-med beasts rocking 4.0's. They've recently been getting more into philanthropy by holding a new annual event as well as some smaller projects, such as a weekly tutoring program in North St. Louis. In the end though, what makes these guys different isn't their philanthropy or some frosting like that, it's that they don't take themselves too seriously and they let people be themselves. If you're looking for a fraternity full of really smart, good-looking, socially conscious athletes, this probably isn't the right spot as they have their fare share of goofy idiots (any fraternity who can't realize the value of a goofy idiot is no fraternity worth being in). On the other hand, if you're looking for a laid back bunch of guys to spend four wild years with, then you've found them.

A hater of this house would say: Hi, my name is_____ and I'm a Sigma Chi pledge.

Most likely Seen Wearing: Mustache and bell bottoms.

Guys Rushing:
Often Consider: Sammy, SAE, AEPi
Sometimes Consider: AEPi
Rarely Consider: Phi Delt, Kappa Sig

Sammy

If Jesus, Gandhi, Abe Lincoln and Charles Barkley went to Wash. U., they'd probably be in Sammy (Sigma Alpha Mu), or at least party with them off campus when finished with the whole civil disobedience thing.

A fan of this house might say: There's something special about this frat, but I just can't place it. Maybe it's because Sammy has no solid flavor - each member brings something different. The brotherhood is the only one that can unite budding New York financiers with Birkenstock wearing backwoods hippies. What unites Sammy brothers is a constant drive to get down - to finish work, kick back, party hard, and create some new adventure in their off-campus world. Don't get it twisted - Sammy held the highest GPA of any greek organization on campus for countless consecutive years (though they dropped from this position last year), even recognized nationally. But Sammys chill like none other. After recent trouble with the school, Sammy has re-grounded and relocated itself off-campus, and is quickly becoming more noticeable on campus. Unlike some other fraternities, Sammy never turns people down at the door when it comes to partying or even on nights off when people just want to hang out and get to know some brothers. While Sammys often move at the pace of a sloth, they will get their shit done in time to celebrate anything worth celebrating, even if it's just a Wednesday.

A hater of this house might say: Well, they don't even have a house, and they are the most lazy, apathetic people on campus. Their New York Jews only want to read the Wall Street Journal and their hippies don't shower. One of them threw up on my wall, did a keg stand, and threw up again, while the other Sammys cheered him on...it was horrible!

Most likely seen wearing: Tie-dye Phish shirt for the 3rd day in a row or polos with pea coats.

Guys rushing...
Often Consider: ZBT, SAE
Sometimes Consider: SigEp, Phi Delt
Rarely Consider: Theta Xi, Sigma Chi

Sigma Nu

Testimonials for Sigma Nu:
"Is it just me or does everyone in Sigma Nu look like dinosaurs." –JuicyCampus (defunct)
"Never going to let you down... Never going to tell a lie and hurt you..." –Rick Astley
"They are fine." –CollegeACB

A fan of this house might say: Sigma Nu's, often found in House #2 on Fraternity Row, are a fairly diverse group. Most guys are involved in a wide range of activities outside of greek life – ranging from UTrucking and Varsity Sports to helping build charter schools for underprivileged kids. The common thread seems to be the "nice guy" label, which they take pride in. Because the house is on upper row, they have a slightly smaller house, which has led the walls to literally melt on particularly lively and well-attended social gatherings. Several guys in the house are DJs, who can be seen spinning away during their typical blacklight parties. In the Greek community, Sigma Nu is especially involved in Philanthropy and Intramurals, having won the Burmeister with Delta Gamma at the Thurtene Carnival three out of the past five years and consistently placing in the top 4 in the Fraternity Intramural league.

A hater of this house might say: If you buy into a strict social hierarchy (and all the cool kids do), extensive research on CollegeACB seems to put Sigma Nu in the middle of the pack with great variability either way amongst especially vocal anonymous users. The guys in Sigma Nu (publically) never really claim to be anything else: a group of solid guys who party until the walls melt. And who look like dinosaurs. Apparently.

Most likely seen wearing: UV3's

Guys Rushing...
Often Consider: Theta Xi, Beta
Sometimes Consider: Sigma Chi, Kappa Sig
Rarely Consider: SigEp, Phi Delt

Greek Life

Theta Xi

Theta Xi (The Taxi) is coming fresh off of summer break and swinging back into full force. With homecoming just around the corner, the brothers are looking forward to their annual pig roast in front of the house.

A Fan of this house might say: They are such a laid back brotherhood, on any random day you can catch someone grilling out on the porch or just simply hanging out outside. With the second highest Greek GPA on campus, the brothers study as hard as they party, which is always a good thing. Although there is no common reputation that brings the brothers together, it can still be said to have one of the strongest brotherhoods on campus. If you are willing to give them a chance, they might surprise your expectations.

A hater of this house might say: The diversity of the brothers gives it an Animal House feel. With no real reputation and constantly a mess, it is only a good place to go and get a free beer. Social interactions are not really their strong point but that's OK, we still love them.

Most likely seen wearing: Chauffer uniform.

Guys rushing...
Often Consider: Kappa Sig, Sigma Nu
Sometimes Consider: Sigma Chi, TKE, Beta
Rarely Consider: ZBT, Sammy, Phi Delt

TKE

A Fan of this house might say: If you build it they will come. TKE is known as the engineering frat, because well, most of the brothers are engineers, so they can build a lot of cool stuff. They have a light up dance floor and one of their alumni used to compete in international beard competitions.

A hater of this house might say: Well these guys are the only ones who did not write up their own article which speaks for itself. They usually scavenge freshmen who can't get into SigEp parties when they fill up, and they had an alumni who competed in an international beard competition.

Most likely seen wearing: USB drive and tool belt.

Guys rushing...
Often Consider: Theta Xi, Beta
Sometimes Consider: AEPi, SigNu
Rarely Consider: Sammy, SigEp

Greek Life

Wash. U.phamisms:

17) *Upper Row - p., Upper row is home to the oldest fraternity houses on campus: Sig Nu, Sigma Chi, Kappa Sig, Phi Delt, Theta Xi and SAE. Resting just beside the AC and behind the law school in the West-most of campus.*

18) *Lower row- p., Below the upper row and peppered between Northside campus housing (Village House, Lopata House, Millbrook Apartments). Home to Sig Ep, TKE, AEPi, and Beta.*

Wash. U.
Sororities

Greek Life

Sororities

*Editor's note: As we said, there was a lot of trouble getting the sororities to write much of anything for us. Instead of writing something for them we picked out quotes from each chapters Wash. U. website or nationals website. To spice things up we also added an interactive section. See if you can match the sorority with the appropriate Sesame Street character (no answers provided).

1.___ Kappa Kappa Gamma *aka Kappa*

"In Kappa I have found friends who make me laugh, who challenge me, and who I know will always be there for me. I have found an opportunity to grow as an individual and as a leader. In Kappa I have found a wonderful lifelong experience"

Philanthropy event: Kappa Kareoke (Reading is Fundamental/Lydia's House)

2.___ Alpha Epsilon Phi *aka AEPhi*

"The mission of Alpha Epsilon Phi Sorority is to inspire and support exemplary women dedicated to friendship and a lifelong commitment to Alpha Epsilon Phi while building on the vision of our Jewish founders"

Philanthropy event: Phi Pheast (Elizabeth Glaser Pediatric AIDS Foundation)

3.___ Pi Beta Phi *aka Pi Phi*

"As a member of Pi Beta Phi, you will discover a home away from home on your campus! Let Pi Beta Phi come alongside you as you discover your passions and dreams during the most formative years of your life"

Philanthropy event: Down and Dirty (Links for Literacy)

4.___ Chi Omega *aka Chi O*

"Whether we are making memories on a Sisterhood Retreat, apple-

Sororities

picking at Eckert's Farm, or hosting a movie night with group of sisters, the friends we make in Chi Omega will stand with us throughout our entire lives"

Philanthropy event: Adopt-A-Dog (Make-A-Wish Foundation)

5.___ Alpha Omicron Pi *aka AOPi*

AOPi was brought to Wash. U., in 2009, making it the youngest sorority on campus. "AOΠ's have crush parties, date events, and mixers, as well as many informal hang outs with just sisters, like movies in the suite or dinner in the Central West End."

Philanthropy event: Strike Out Arthritis (Arithritis Research)

6.___ Alpha Phi *aka A Phi*

"Alpha Phi is dedicated to promoting sisterhood, cultivating leadership, advocating service, and encouraging intellectual curiosity...Our chapter is a close-knit group of amazing, passionate, genuine women, active both in our chapter and in all areas of campus life."

Philanthropy event: Phi Ball (Alpha Phi Foundation)

7.___ Delta Gamma *aka DG*

"Delta Gamma's Alpha Epsilon chapter at Washington University began as 'The Shrine of the Mystic Seven' in 1907... With the addition of each new pledge class, Delta Gamma hopes to continue to make a positive impact on Washington University"

Philanthropy event: Anchor Splash (Service for Sight)

Sororities

a. Big Bird
Cheery and bright, this loveable bird is known for his exuberant attitude as well as his large beak.

b. Cookie Monster
Although some may consider him a cookie horder, this harmless blue critter is generous and kind at heart, but he'll fuck you up if you stick your hand in his cookie jar.

c. Grouch
Although his outfits may appear trashy, this character knows how to have fun in any situation.

d. Elmo
Tickle at your own risk.

e. Bert
Ernie's responsible life partner, Bert is known as one of the the smartest people you'll meet, which isn't surprising when you consider the dimensions of his head.

f. Ernie
Just because he's orange doesn't mean he fake bakes. Ernie is one of the kindest kids on the street, so if he asks you for a favor, know that he'll reciprocate ;)

g. Snuffleupagus - Always
looking to get cozy, Snuffy's goofy demeanor complements his beady eyes and sensitive trunk.

160

Not Going Greek

Freshman year I wasn't able to rush and I was sure this was going to ruin my Wash. U. experience. All of my friends joined sororities and I had always pictured myself in one. I got a chance to rush in the fall of my sophomore year and could have chosen to go through recruitment in the spring. However, by that time I decided it wasn't worth it, and I don't regret the decision one bit. Though I must admit, there have been times where I watched my Greek friends get ready for their formals, get candy and gifts from their pledge mothers, and felt just a little jealous over not being in a sorority. At first, not going Greek felt like having fewer friends, having fewer social events, and not knowing as many frat guys. However, by the time my sophomore year ended, not going Greek meant not having to work countless hours at the ThurtenE Lot, and not going to long meetings with candle passes talking about the emotions of people I'm not friends with, crying, and over- enthusiastic cheering. It may be different for fraternities, but sororities at Wash. U. are not so close that any girl only has friends in their sorority; they are huge and don't have houses. I'll often hear a girl say, "Oh yea, I think she's in my sorority..." Sisters? I don't need to pay hundreds of dollars to be sisters with girls whose names I don't even know.

There are two things that I was worried not going Greek would affect: friendships and social life. It has affected neither. Most, if not all of my close friends are Greek, and the girls that I live with are all in different sororities. Joining a Greek organization is a good way to gather a large number of acquaintances, and make a small number of close friends. But you don't need to be greek to do the same. Socially, there is a "Greek" scene at Wash. U. Everyone in it seems to know each other and everyone seems to be Greek. But you don't actually have to be Greek to be in that scene, and you definitely don't have to be in that scene to party or have an active social life. There are enough organizations, sport teams, acapella groups and other clubs that are just as tight-knit as sororities to have an exciting social life. While it may be a tough decision for some people to go Greek, either way you will have an amazing experience.

Greek Life

VII

Wash. U.

Social Life

"You have four years to be irresponsible here. Relax. Work is for people with jobs. You'll never remember class time, but you'll remember time you wasted hanging out with your friends. So, stay out late. Go out on a Tuesday with your friends when you have a paper due Wednesday. Spend money you don't have. Drink 'til sunrise. The work never ends, but college does...""

-Tom Petty

W.I.L.D.

Walk In Lay Down

W.I.L.D. is Wash. U.'s day-long concert and festival commemorating the start and end of the school year. What started as a small picnic and movie festival more than 35 years ago has now become the largest and most anticipated student-run event of the year. For the school community, W.I.L.D. not only represents a time to enjoy great music but a time to relax and party with friends. Put aside all preconceptions about what you think your W.I.L.D. will be like. You are promised to find a surprise or two, anything from giveaways at the door, to local catered barbecue, to a new favorite artist.

Since its inception, Team 31 Productions has organized and produced the event at no cost for the 12,000+ members of the Wash. U. community. Planning begins months before each show, when the student board is selected and the talent search begins. With a budget based solely on an allocation from Student Union, the two shows require detailed and careful spending on stage set up, quad security, groundskeeping, and food before booking any talent. Without the funds to secure someone of arena caliber, Team 31 turns its attention towards rising talent and nationally recognized mid-level acts, with an emphasis on live performance and crowd control. Staffed with experts of the music scene, Team 31 is a group we can believe in. Wash. U. students often have the privilege of seeing an artist before they are famous, which brings the ever important musical bragging rights over their friends. While everyone cannot be pleased upon first hearing the lineup, each act earns its spot after great consideration from the board. Each year when the line-up is announced there is a collective shout of joy or a begrudging moan. No matter what the initial reaction is, the show never disappoints. As long as students keep an open mind, and come to the show ready to hear some awesome tunes, W.I.L.D is guaranteed to be one of the greatest days of the year. Recent acts include Talib Kweli, Passion Pit, Lupe Fiasco, Method Man and Red Man, Major Lazer and Wale. Spring 2011's W.I.L.D. featured Flying Lotus and Edward Sharpe and the Magnetic Zeros

In addition to W.I.L.D., Team 31 Productions sponsors a number of events including a Second Stage for student talent to showcase their talents at as well as a DJ battle to find Wash. U. a student to perform in between acts at W.I.L.D.

Social Life

W.I.L.D.- A "Different" Perspective

Disclaimer- WILD is one of the most fun days of the year. Please be safe. Follow your best judgment, even if it is impaired, and if you think you've had too much to drink then you have probably had too much to drink. Again, if you or your friends is truly in trouble remember of the Fist Full of Fives or call 935-5555.

The most important part about W.I.L.D. however is not the music, as will become painfully obvious within seconds of waking up on that glorious day during the fall semester. W.I.L.D. is the one day of the year where everyone, I mean everyone, (and by I mean everyone I mean a small percentage of the school, but a larger than the normal party crowd) get hammered beyond recognition. The school has tried to cut back on this, but as it is nearly impossible, they provide an emergency tent in the quad for people who drink too much and need to regurgitate a few meals, or just feel sleepy and want a place to rest. Before W.I.L.D. it is customary to funnel and shotgun as many times as possible while always keeping a side beer in your back pocket. You may also meet a bag of Franzia which you will be inclined to slap after chugging a bit, or even a bottle of classless Sterling Vodka which should be avoided every other day except for W.I.L.D., as there is no such thing as being classy on W.I.L.D. Fraternities will have fantastic pregames as will the off campus community, but don't be afraid to get rowdy in the dorm. Your RA's will have a conversation with you about drinking on W.I.L.D., and you should take it to heart. But no matter what they say, if you happen to run into them on W.I.L.D., don't expect them to remember. Because the sign that you had a good W.I.L.D. is that you don't remember being there. Or that you didn't even make it to the quad.

School Parties
Oxymoron? You be the judge

Vertigo

Vertigo is the night those genius engineers put their education to good use and throw together a sweet party. Known for its light-up dance floor and quirky theme, the scene is fun but for the most part appeals to underclassmen. It's always a good time but be ready for a lot of people in a small, extremely hot space with lots of flashing lights.

Bauhaus

Every year the art/architecture schools throw together a nice little shindig around the time of Halloween. Built on the parking lot in front of Givens Hall, a massive tent glows with strobe lights and shakes with bass. It's a good time, and if you come dressed in a good costume, you will realize it's also a good place meet a friend for the night. There is a maximum capacity in the tent and tickets sell out fast, so jump on the bandwagon early and snag one to attend of the better on-campus parties of the year.

Art Prom

The formal of ridiculousness, Art Prom is the art schools biggest annual social. Held in April just before finals, this party is a great way to de-stress before exams begin. Students are expected to dress up in a mixture shiny, pleathery, neony, clothing, and then rage the night away.

Wash. U. Goggles

It's December, and you have now been at school for four months. As you walk around campus, glancing at students dressed for the tundra, something strange happens... People begin to look attractive to you! Below the sweatpants, winter jackets, and chapped lips, you begin to find outer beauty. This is a sensation you haven't felt since the first week of school! What's happening? How can this be?

Don't be scared my child, for there is a simple explanation for this phenomenon. You have unknowingly stumbled upon a pair of 100% authentic Wash. U. goggles. You might not feel them pulled down over your eyes, but they are there as surely as the sky is blue, the grass is green, and the kappa is blonde.

You get to school and see everything through a beautiful pair of freshman minted rose colored glasses. Everyone and everything is beautiful. For the next few weeks you are living in a state of bliss. Parties every night, people want to talk to you, and floorcest is rampant. As the semester progresses, your vision is slowly corrected as students begin to swap booze for books. People lose interest in that one fun fact you saved up for the ice breaker games, and floorcest begins to tear apart that once divine fabric that kept your floor together. This painful fall from Cloud 9 is accompanied by the realization that people at Wash. U. are just not that attractive. At first, this may send you into a tumbling depression of despair, shakes, and drug addiction. But fear not my friend, all is not lost!

You struggle through the rest of the semester, lost in a sea of monotony, and then, as quickly as your delusions melted away, a sparkle returns to life. Wash. U. goggles is the endearing term used to describe the unique mental state where one consciously or unconsciously changes their perception of the world to accommodate for the sub par attractiveness of the student body at Washington University. The name is derived from the well known "Beer Goggles," which is used to explain why drunk people wake up next to wildabeast the morning after a big night. Wash. U. goggles only differ in the sense that once you put them on, they don't come off until you return home for winter or summer break, get a job, visit another school, watch TV, read a magazine, look at your friends facebooks, etc. Beware of combining Wash. U. goggles with Beer goggles. You might make decisions that haunt you for the rest of your college career.

It hurts to talk about this, but the truth hurts. Some of you may throw your hands up to the Big Guy upstairs and ask why you are being punished, but once you can accept the fact that you need the goggles to survive, your time at Wash. U. could just be the college experience you've always dreamed of.

Alcohol

Underground Guide to Wash. U.

Despite Wash. U.'s rigorous workload and the stresses that go along with it, the school has a surprisingly lax alcohol policy. Starting on day one as a freshman, RAs explain a "red flag" alcohol policy in which students are, for the most part, allowed to drink responsibly as long as it is not dangerous or disruptive. Drinking games fall under both dangerous and disruptive, so if you get caught playing one in your dorm there could be consequences. And if a student's drinking becomes too repetitive or flagrant, that is if the school notices a student being too repetitive or flagrant, the University will take action. Yet serious judicial consequences from alcohol consumption alone are rare, and Wash. U.'s alcohol policy creates a student-to-RA relationship that is often casual, open, and honest.

It should be of no surprise that students have a high level of comfort with having and drinking alcohol in their rooms on a regular basis. Despite the fact that many students prefer lifestyles without alcohol, many still enjoy anything from the casual brew to the Wednesday-Saturday drinking marathon. Wash. U. is no state school, and its drinking scene cannot compare by any stretch of the imagination, but that doesn't mean we don't like to party.

So how do you get your hands on this mystical substance? The South 40 is within walking distance of Schnucks, a supermarket that is also the closest source of alcohol. In recent years, however, the University administration has become aware of the vast student population with fake IDs and their frequent visits to this 24-hour Schnucks. Although it is rare to get caught with a fake at this supermarket, many students won't take the risk since they will inform the school if they do. In addition, while the University seems to take responsible drinking lightly, the administration has little tolerance for use of a fake ID.

Many students will make the trek to the next closest Schnucks in University City, just a short 2-minute drive away. While they have a smaller selection, they still have the $10 handles of liquor that get the job done just as well as Goose, and they provide a much more pleasant buying experience. Getting the alcohol back to your room is as easy as putting it in a bag and walking right in (it must be hidden from plain sight). If it's concealed as such, you could walk right by the Chancellor's office without fear.

Although you will have no problem getting drunk in your room or pre-gaming for a fraternity party, the school has been getting stricter with flagrant drunkenness in public. Should your stomach decide you've

Social Life

had enough to drink before your brain, keep it to a bathroom or a nice bush out of plain sight. If you get sick in public there will most likely be repercussions that depend on your specific "crime" and your record. Punishments can range from making an alcohol-education poster to community service or even counseling. The administration does not want you throwing up or tossing beer cans everywhere after a party, just to be seen by next morning's admissions tour. In that respect, feel free to get alcohol, drink it, go to a fraternity party, drink some more, but just be smart about it. The Wash. U. police department (WUPD) is here to protect you, not arrest you—many students even know some WUPD officers on a personal level. But, they'll have no problem writing you up if you've gone too far.

Things get a little different off-campus. For the most part, on-campus is a much safer place to drink. On the WUPD controlled campus, you will not be written up for simply being drunk, even if it is visible. They only take action if someone is visibly sick or out of control. However, just one street north of campus, this wonderful freedom all but disappears. Crossing over the bridge you enter University City—a small "city" which encompasses a large area of off-campus residences and the vast majority of off-campus parties. This residential neighborhood consists of almost an equal number of students and local families that have been there for generations, and neither group seems to be leaving anytime soon. A rather unfriendly student-family resident relationship has evolved over the past year, which has escalated into a new "zero-tolerance" policy that has forced local University Police to arrest undergraduates for even the slightest crime. Noise complaints, whether for a big party, small party, or no party, are now justification for student arrests. Having an open container of alcohol has caused a University City arrest as well. Though the University has made strides in the last year to build a relationship between students, there is still a long way to go.

One thing the RAs will certainly explain is the University's Emergency Service Team (EST). EST is the school's student-run team of volunteer responders to a medical emergency that runs 24/7. It is confidential, and the University asks that students feel free to call EST if they feel a student is seriously sick. Without a doubt, it is a great service to have on campus in the event of a true emergency, as it provides a solution for students who might have otherwise not felt comfortable with calling for an ambulance. If you even suspect that someone is in trouble you should immediately call EST. Any potential consequences by the school are nothing compared to what can happen if someone has had too much to drink.

Wash. U. is in a unique situation right now, as it is quickly becoming the "next Ivy." Today, we can easily compete with Cornell or UPenn in terms of academic rigor. But Wash. U. has only attained this elite status recently. Only in this generation has Wash. U. become such a prestigious school, and the administration is accordingly becoming evermore worried with its image. As a whole, Wash. U. still has an extremely fair alcohol policy that will only get in your way if something obviously flagrant happens; it is the growing off-campus problem that is hurting students in the long run. Likewise, because the administration is keeping a sharp eye out for the University's image, interfering with off-campus authorities has been a touchy subject, and progress is minimal for both sides. Nevertheless, Wash. U. still has a relatively accepting "red flag" policy that allows freshman to get and drink alcohol with ease, but within reason. As much as students may have disdain for the overbearing off-campus enforcement, very few complain about the University's alcohol policy. It lets you buy, it lets you drink, and it even lets you get drunk. Very few universities, especially of this rigor, let their RAs witness a student come home wasted and simply make sure he or she gets in bed safely. The Beastie Boys said it best: You gotta fight for your right to party.

Wash. U.phamisms:

19) Forsyth- p., Street splitting main campus from the 40. You can take it west towards Clayton and some off campus fraternity houses and east towards Forest Park

20) Duffy's - With kareokee on Tuesdays and trivia on Wednesdays, this bar regularly attracts a solid mid-week party crew. Located next to the Clayton Schnucks, Duffy's is not only extremely close to campus, it also has cheap pitchers of very cheap beer so you can quench your thirst for liquid courage before bellowing Rick Astley into the microphone in front of 50 Wash. U. students.

Wash. U.phamisms:

21) Anorexic Bunny - n., The only outdoor piece of artwork on upper campus. Students cannot go a day without passing it between classes. It gets its name due to the severe lack of nutrition the poor sculpture of a bunny seems to have.

22) The Swamp-p., Grassy area in the center of the 40. While recent construction has dramatically reduced the size of the swamp, it still has a volleyball court, basketball courts, and a field for football, ultimate, etc. Host to the annual event Holi, and a comfortable sleeping place for drunks in the beginning and end of the year.

Wash. U.

Drinking Games

Beer Pong

No, the real Beer Pong

At Wash. U., people often get confused with the difference between Beirut and Beer Pong. The answer lies in the difference between the titles themselves. Beer pong is the game that closely resembles ping pong with the use of paddles and ping pong balls.

Legend has it that in the early 1950s, two Dartmouth fraternity brothers were playing ping pong while drinking beer (a stand up idea on its own), when one put his cup down on the table and the other hit it in. Like the moment when the apple hit Newton on the head, a beautiful idea was born: modern competitive drinking games. Dartmouth still plays the game religiously today, shunning all those who mistakenly refer to Beirut as Beer Pong.

Setup: The game may be played singles or doubles depending on whether two or four people are present. For basic singles, one would take a full cup of beer and place it one paddle-width away from the base/back line of the table aligned with the vertically central line. At Dartmouth, and also in places where there are some legit pong players, the eight cup or 14 cup "Christmas Tree" setup is used. Also, for true pong, handles should be broken off the paddles, and the paddles should be wood on both side (grip is neither allowed nor advised).

Rules:

1. One team does a regular ping pong serve--the ball must be a blatant lob off of the bounce and all balls must be hit upward after (laser shots are not allowed).

2. If you hit a cup off of the serve, you take a penalty drink of half a cup.

3. If you hit a cup, the opponent must drink half of the cup in question. A player may attempt to save the cup after the ball hits a cup by returning it, with the standard lob (providing the ball doesn't bounce on his side of the court more than once). If he doesn't save it, he drinks half the cup, and starts the next point by serving in the same way the game was started.

172

4. If the ball goes into one of the cups, that player must drink the remaining beer and the cup is removed. The winning team is the one who eliminates their opponents' cups while retaining at least one cup of their own.

5. EXTRA—knocking over a cup will result in a penalty chug. Just drink the salvageable beer left after the knock over, fill the cup back up to the brim, and continue play.

6. The standard size for pong cups are 10oz. clear cups, which are typically difficult to find in your average store.

7. When trying to save a cup that has been hit, a player is allowed to use his body to intercept the wild ball before returning the ball back. Note: if the defending player uses his body, the ball can still only bounce a total of one time on his side that turn.

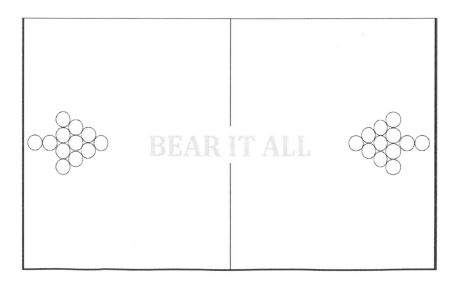

Drinking Games

Beirut

The Quintessential College Experience

Beirut, improperly referred to as Beer Pong, is a time tested college tradition. It is a game which requires skill, focus, and stamina. It also can bring out the competitive edge of even the most quiet and reserved players. It is a simple game, which merely requires players to throw ping pong balls into Solo cups on opposite ends of a table. However, the game has many variations, and most players feel strongly about their own rules.

Typically games are played with 10 cups on each end (base four), but some play with twelve (two side-by-side base three pyramids). According to BPONG.COM the standard table length is 8' x 2', however, most college students play on any surface they can find (try a door on top of a few stacked bins).

The first point of contention you will find among Beirut enthusiasts is how to treat a cup that has been made. It is common practice to leave the cup, so that if it is made again in the same turn, the defending side must drink three cups. Others play that if you hit the same cup twice (both with beer in them) you "Beiruted" your opponent, and they instantly lose.

Some other rules that are typical at WU are:

•**Naked Lap**: The naked lap is enforced when a team loses with a certain number of cups remaining. Some rules require a naked lap if all 10 of the losing teams cups remain. Others deem a naked lap with any number of cups greater than six.

•**Penn State Rules**: A popular way to make games go quickly. If you shoot and miss the table you have to drink one of your own cups.

•**Bounce Rules**: If you are too busy flirting with the person next to you to notice a bounce - or too inebriated to slap the ball away - you must drink two of your own cups.

•**Troll Rule**: If a player on the losing team makes zero cups, he is the designated "troll" for the following game. He must sit under the table with the case of beer and must hand beers to anybody who needs them until the next game is complete.

•**Fire\NBA Jams**: Refers to when a player makes three consecutive shots, they go "On Fire" similar to the classic video game NBA Jam. That player can then shoot until they miss. Most people require the person to declare that they are "Heating up" (when 2 cups are hit in a row) which is also from the video game.

•**Send Backs**: A very common rule which states that if both players on the team make a shot on a given turn they get both the balls back to shoot again.

•**1, 2 Step**: This rule refers to the situation when both players make the last cup on a given turn. The other team then immediately loses the game without a chance of rebuttal.

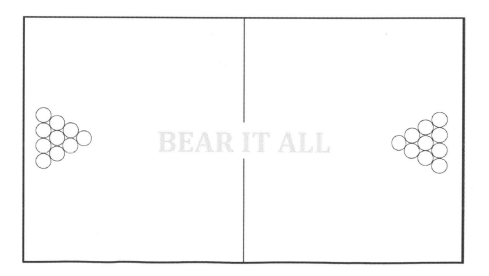

Drinking Games

Defend Your Castle
It's like a board game...with drinking

Set up: 24 cups, 12 quarters, 2 ping-pong balls, 4 human-beings (2 teams of 2)

Place 4 cups at each corner of the table. Put about three shots of the liquor of choice in the corner edge cup while filling the other cups with half a beer. The edge is your throne, the surrounding cups are your wall. Place 4 cups in a vertical line on each side, with the last one touching the table's edge, and fill with less than half a beer. These are your troops. Each player gets 3 quarters to put in the wall cups. Decide who goes first by a game of bloody knuckles (very much optional, a game of paper-scissors rock will do just fine).

Play:

There are three ways to win.
   1. Hitting both of the thrones of the opposing team with ping-pong balls.

   2. Having one cup in your troops line touch the middle/ net of the table.

   3. Throwing a quarter into one of the thrones of the opposing team.

Each turn, teams take two shots with the ping-pong balls. If a troops cup is hit, it is fully consumed and removed from the table. If the throne is hit, the castle owner must drink his throne cup only and is out of the game. After every team's turn, their back cup moves directly to the forward of the line so that eventually, if not hit, the line will cross the center and the game will be won. If cups in the middle of the troops' line are hit, the cups in front up it are shifted back to cover the space making a solid line of cups once more.

Quarters signify an extra life, so if a wall cup is hit, the quarter is removed and the wall cup is moved to the back (closer) of the troops line. That quarter may now be used by that team to shoot with, in addition to the two ping-pong ball shots. One team has as many shots as they have number of quarters + 2 ping-pong balls. If a quarter is thrown into a wall cup, that cup is placed at the back of the line with 2 lives, one for each quarter.

The game is one of strategic play-making and aggressive beer and liquor drinking. It's not advisable to play this game in a dorm room unless you're sleeping with your CA or at least have very strong brotherly bonds with him. Think and enjoy responsibly.

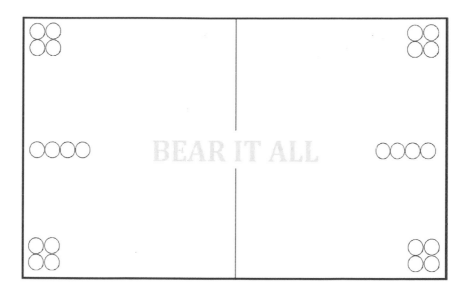

Wash. U.phamisms:
23) Bird Call (this might not exist anymore)- cl., When the pasta line runs out of fried chicken, the pasta man emits the bird call to replenish his stocks.
24) Village Brunch- cl., Some would say the best meal a man can get on campus. Served on weekends in the Village, brunch offers everything from pancakes to breakfast sandwiches. It seems to be just the trick for any given hangover...

Drinking Games

Flipcup

Competitive, yet social

Flipcup is a game that rivals Beirut in popularity. It is played exclusively in parties. Flipcup is by far the easiest drinking game but can get increasingly hard as you drink more and more. The game is popular because an unlimited amount of people can play at once. Flipcup is also extremely simple. When looking for a game that more than four people can play at a time Flipcup is a very good choice.

Set up:

1. A cup for every person playing (Plastic cups only)

2. Enough beer to fill every cup at least 1/4 full

3. A table with room for every person to place a cup

Flipcup generally requires at least 6 players. As many can play as desired as long as there are an even number of players. Solo Party cups are the preferred cup of Flipcup but others can be substituted. The beer should be light, as you will have to chug it as fast as possible.

Rules:
1. Two teams with an equal number of members line up on opposite sides of a table. Everyone should have at least 1/4 cup filled with beer. Some players may choose to add more beer but this is a personal choice. To make sure there are and even number of people, all players are required to raise and touch cups with the person matching them on the opposite team.

2. The game begins at one end of the table. The first two players touch cups in the air. There are different ways to start the game but the most simple is to count to three together. The first players must then touch the bottom of their cups to the table before they begin drinking. Once the cups hit the table they chug the beer as fast as they can. Once they've finished their beer, the players place their cups at the edge of the table so that one end is hanging off the edge. The object of the game is to flip the cup over using one hand and get it to land with the mouth facing down. You are not allowed to touch the cup with the other hand unless to reset it for another flip.

3. Once the player before you manages to flip their cup over, you begin the same routine. You are not allowed to pick your cup up off the table before the player in front of you has successfully flipped their cup.

4. The game ends when all members of one team have flipped their cups.

5. When beginning the next game start with the next pair of opposing players in line. The game would then end with the pair who started the last round. Flip cup does not take much practice and should be relatively easy for beginners.

Some tricks people use is placing a can behind your cup before you flip it. This creates a backboard so the cup does not flip extra times. Another trick is to wet the surface under your cup. This creates a small amount of suction when the mouth lands on the table. It shouldn't be hard to find a game of Flip Cup at any party, and if there isn't one don't be afraid to start one.

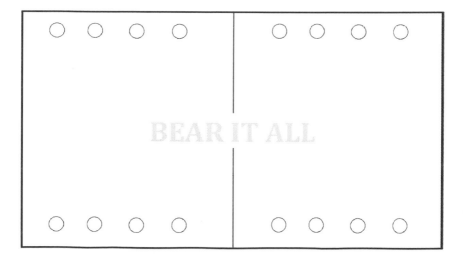

Drinking Games

BeiFlip

A hybrid of two favorites

BeiFlip is an alternative drinking game that allows the competitive guys and girls to play both Beirut and Flipcup in the same game.

Played on any surface that Beirut can be played, BeiFlip can accommodate any even number of players--making it an excellent game for a group of people at a party looking to get hammered together. The game consists of two teams, each with a triangle with base three or four at opposite ends. One person from each team starts as the shooter, taking the first Beirut shot at the other team's cups. The rest of the teams are lined up along the table, each with a 1/4-1/2 filled cup of beer in front of them. If a cup is made, the flip cup game begins at the end of the table where the cup was made. The team whose cup is made acts as the defending team, meaning if their team wins the flipcup game, they successfully defend their cup and the cup that was made is not drank and remains as part of the game.

Specifics:

-The game can be played with either triangles of base 3 or 4, depending on how long everyone is willing to play
-More intense players choose to fill their flipcups halfway or more
-There is no send-backs or "On Fire" in BeiFlip
-Ideally, all participants play the whole game without substitutions
-15 beers are a minimum for this game, don't attempt to play with less
-After shooting, the shooter rotates to the end of the flipcup line and the next player steps up to shoot
-The shooter in a particular turn never flips himself

Do not get frustrated if your first attempts end in failure. After all, even the losers of a drinking game win. Make sure to put a towel across the crack under your dorm room door.

This game requires a complex set up, but for all you smarty-pants who care to play a true strategic game of drinking, this is a splendid choice. Listen carefully to the setup and game play. You are the King trying to defend your throne. Care for your troops, protect your walls, don't let the opposing kingdom strip you from your royal status.

Wizard Staff
... Did he just get avada kedavara'd?

One of the simplest games in existence, yet one of the most fun. Wizard Staff can quickly turn your average Tuesday night into a massive drunken L.A.I.R. battle ground. When you have nothing lying around but some beer and a roll of duct tape, wizard staff should be your game of choice.

Set up:

Buy your beer. Find a roll of Duct Tape.

Gameplay:

1. Drink your first beer

2. Get your second beer and duct tape it to the top of your first beer. Drink your second beer.

3. Get your third beer and duct tape it to the top of your second beer. Drink your third beer.

4. Repeat until the beer runs out.

By the end you will have created what resembles a wizard staff. The winner of the game is the person with the biggest staff. As your staff grows, it will probably start to bend. The key of this game is to do a careful job when taping the cans together, making sure that you create nice even rings that keep the cans vertical. When you really can't think of any reason to drink, this friendly game will fend off your friends who have been calling you an alcoholic, at least for the night.

Power Hour

...Keep taking baby steps

In one hour you are supposed to be at a sorority date function. Don't panic, that's plenty of time to convince yourself that you actually got invited by a cute girl. By convince yourself I mean fill your stomach with liquid confidence and self delusion. The Power-Hour is a great way to pregame with beer and a lot of people.

Set Up: Get a shot glass for every person that will be participating. Create a playlist with 60 songs each lasting one minute. Alternatively find a pre-made power hour playlist somwhere online.

Gameplay:

1. Fill your shot glass with beer and hit play on the iPod and take that shot.

2. While the song is playing refill your glass and hang out for the next minute.

3. When the song changes take your next shot and refill it again.

4. Keep going until the hour is up and the playlist is over.

By the time the power hour has ended, if you kept pace the entire time, you will have drank seven and a half beers. It gets pretty rough towards the end, but if you can "power" through, you will be rewarded with super human strength and attractiveness. For the fratty folks out there, don't be afraid to keep a side beer if the shots aren't enough.

Variations include:
Half power hour: 30 shots per 30 minutes Century Club: 100 shots per 100 minutes Double Trouble: 120 shots per 120 minutes.

(If you are feeling ambitious you can do all of these variations with movie clips instead of songs)

Quarters

Now, there are various way to play this game, but in every condition, you will be drinking, and you will be drinking quickly.

Set Up: You can play with as little as 3 people, however at least 5 or 6 is highly advised and encouraged. Every player sits at a table, preferably round, with a beer. You will also need 2 shot glasses (more depending on how fast and deadly you want the game to be).

Gameplay: The shot glasses start at opposite ends of the table. When the game begins, each player with a shot glass in front of them attempts to bounce the quarter off of the table and into the shot glass. If the shot is made, the shot glass is moved to the left. Over time one shot glass is bound to catch up with the other, and if a shot is made so that the person who sits to the left has still not made their shot then that person has to chug.

Icing

Making Smirnoff Ice cool since 2010

No one knows exactly how this phenomenon started. Some people say it was a bunch of students at Charleston who thought it up, others believe the marketing geniuses at Smirnoff covertly spread this game to increase their sales. Either way, Icing has taken The States by storm, and made drinking Smirnoff Ice socially acceptable, and maybe even cool.

Set Up: Get Smirnoff Ice

Gameplay: Present the Smirnoff to your friend and say "Iced!" Your friend must now take a knee and chug the entire bottle. However, if your friend has an Ice on him, he blocks your Ice, and you must then get down on a knee and chug the Ice. The fun of this game comes from the various ways you present the Ice. You can leave it in their desk drawer, put it in their backpack, or have a bartender give it to them when they order a drink. Anything goes. The Ice must be chugged no matter what time of day.

Rumors have it that an employee of Goldman Sachs was Iced on the trading floor, as well as Screech from Saved By The Bell and Keenan & Kel theme song rapper, Coolio.

Drinking Games

Baseball
Less boring than actual baseball

If you need a drinking game to play on a slow night, this is the perfect one. The rules are pretty simple and oriented around the rules of Americas favorite past time (no, not shoveling a mouthful of freedom fries in your mouth). To play this game you'll need between 4 and 8 people, preferably an even number.

Set Up: You'll need a table adequate for "beirut" or "beer pong", and a decent amount of space. Each team should have 5 solo cups and four should be set up in a straight line in the middle of the table similar to the straight line in "beirut", these represent a single, double, triple and homerun (from closest to farthest from the opposing team). The final cup should be placed on the side of the table, it doesn't really matter which side or where as long as it's the opposite of the other team's, this is your steal cup. All cups should be filled with the amount of beer appropriate for beirut.

Gameplay:

As you would imagine there are "innings" and each team gets three outs before the other is "batting". While your team is batting you want to score as many runs as possible. You score runs by making cups and advancing players to home base the same way that they would in real baseball. When a cup is made, that cup must be consumed, along with all the cups below it, e.g. if someone hits a triple, the triple, double, and single cups must all be finished. Cups must be refilled after each hit.

The way a team gets an out is if (a) a player shooting misses the cups completely (b) a player strikes out, by hitting the cups 3 times but never actually making one (c) catching them out by catching a ball in the air after it hits a cup and before it hits anything else (d) getting a player out when he attempts to steal. A player can steal when their team has a man on base and all the other cups have been set up and filled with beer. You have to, sneakily if possible, play one

184

cup flipcup with your one steal cup. If you're successful your men on base advance one space, if unsuccessful your lead man is out and no others advance. The exception to this rule is when you are trying to steal home or attempting the suicide squeeze. In this case the same rules apply except you use all 4 of your main cups and your entire team gets involved. You can play for as many innings as you want and the team with the highest score wins. Feel free to get creative with scoreboards and other accessories.

If you hit a homerun make sure to run around the entire room screaming and high fiving team mates.

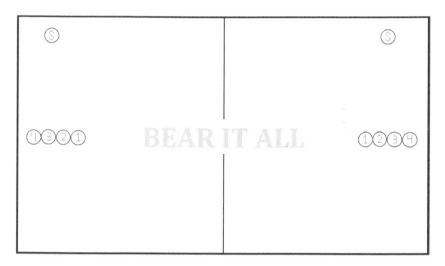

Wash. U.phamisms:

25) U-drive - p., This street rests just on the north side of the overpass, running parallel to Forest Park Parkway. Perhaps the most ideal off-campus housing option for students and is priced accordingly.
26) Kingsbury - p., This street sits 2 blocks south of the loop and tends to house most of the senior off-campus housing community.
27) Wash Ave- p., Street in between Wash. U. and the loop, home to the Greenway Apartments and the lady with the two gigantic bear dogs.

Kings / Ring of Fire

This is a game that is perfect for when you have a good sized group (5 or more) of guys and girls aiming to get very buzzed before the night continues onto Keg Mondays or Deuce Thursdays. There are several variants of the specifics of the game, but the general rules apply for all.

Play: Everyone sits around a table with full can of unopened beer. You start with a deck of cards and a can of unopened beer in the center of the table. One person starts and picks a card from the top of the deck. The person takes the action of the designated card (it's best to write them all out beforehand so there isn't any confusion):

2: "You" -Pick someone to drink

3: "Me" -You drink

4: "Floor" -Last one to touch the floor drinks

5: "Guys" -All guys drink

6: "Chicks" -All girls drink

7: "Heaven" -Last one to point up to the ceiling drinks

8: "Never Have I Ever" -Begins one round of the game

9: "Bust A Rhyme" -Say a sentence. The next player must quickly say a sentence whose last word rhymes with the last word of the first sentence. Continue until someone hesitates. He or she drinks. (Words can only be used once.)

10: "Categories" -the person who drew the card states a general category and says something of that category (i.e. boxers brands, Calvin Klein) and every next person must all say something of the same category until someone fails to do so and drinks.

Jack: "Make a Rule" -this person can make whatever rule they'd like for the table. i.e. You cannot touch your legs or you cannot make eye contact with another. These rules can last until the next Ace is drawn or for the remainder of the game. If somebody violates a rule, they must drink.

Queen: "Questions" -The person who pulls the Queen is Question Master until the next Queen is pulled. He or she can ask a question of another player at any time. If that player answers the question with anything other than another question, he must drink.

King: The first three to pull a King drink when they pull a King.. The game ends when the last King is pulled.

Ace: "Waterfall" -Everyone starts drinking. The person who drew the King can stop when he feels like, and when he does, the next person can stop drinking when he wants, and so on and so on until the last is able to stop.

one drink = one large sip of alcohol

The first player takes that card and puts it inside the tab of the unopened beer in the center. The next person picks a card, follows the instructions for that card, and sticks the card on top of the first card in the tab of the beer in the center. When the tab eventually pops (from continuous playing and sticking cards in the tab) and the beer opens, all must drain their cups. The last to do so must chug the beer in the center. In 3 to 4 rounds of Kings, not only will one enjoy much enjoyment and social conversation, but the individual will also be inebriated enough to make the best "bad" decisions for the rest of the night.

Drinking Games

Wash. U.phamisms:

28) The AC- p., Home to the main basketball courts, swimming pool, cardio room, and weight room. While the sports teams use the weight room to work out, you're more likely to find your 130 lb. roomate benching his orgo textbook.

29) The estrogym - p., This is the gym on the South 40 filled with cardio equipment almost exclusively used by female students. Although this gym is not technically single-sex, 94% of its inhabitants will be wearing some sort of tight-fitting leggings. Men, contrary to your biological intuition, you should NOT come here to hit on girls.

Wash. U.
Going Out

This is a mass text. Does anyone know where I am?

-(401)

Beyond the Wash. U. Bubble
Expanding your horizons in St. Louis

Upon reminiscing about my off-campus social life throughout my college career at Wash. U., I often struggle to pinpoint some of the more outstanding bars, hangouts, and restaurants that have effectively sparked my social curiosity. Perhaps that is the result of the alleged less-than-bubbly social scene within the city of St. Louis, or maybe it is the consequence of prevalent "memory losses" that I experience the morning after partying. In any case, I am hoping for the latter. In all seriousness though, St. Louis offers a wide variety of places to go out and fraternize—you just have to know where to look.

Finding the right place to go out really depends on three things: the night of the week, your mood prior to hitting the town, and the type of people with which you want to mingle. Often times I find myself on Friday night grappling with these social criteria in order to maximize the overall quality of the night. Do I go somewhere traditional where I know my friends will be? Or, do I dare exhibit my social audacity by branching out to a foreign place with an unknown crowd? Whichever way your schmooze sense beckons, hopefully you can expand your party horizons and explore the prime-time bars in some of the more bustling areas of St. Louis.

If you want to go the conventional yet consistent route, Laclede's Landing is your destination. Use your U-Pass for a free ride on the MetroLink. Otherwise, taking a cab costs around $25 leaving from campus. Once you get there, hit up the two Thursday night staples— Morgan Street Brewery and Big Bang. Make sure to capitalize on the $2 pitchers at Morgan Street followed by the debaucherous late-night dueling pianos sing-along at Big Bang. If you feel the need to throw a few back before entering those places, venture into Big Daddy's and Joey B's directly across from Morgan Street. If you are looking for an older, more eclectic crowd, an outdoor drinking patio, and an awesome variety of live music, Broadway Oyster Bar is the place to jam, particularly on Friday nights.

Now maybe you are looking for some classier places to go, perhaps the perfect date spot for you and a significan't other. Bar Napoli in Clayton features an outdoor seating area with a very relaxed atmosphere, and over 20 specialty cocktails. Brennan's in the Central West End is cool, casual, yet still very sophisticated with its selection of wine, whiskey, and scotch. Don't forget about the cigar bar downstairs.

Be careful—drink prices at both these bars are a little steeper, but their respective atmospheres definitely make it worth your dime. If classy isn't really your style, venture out to some of the ever-so-spirited Irish pubs in the area. Kilkenny's in Clayton, albeit a little smaller, always proves to be a fun time when draught Guinness and Irish Car Bombs are flowing all night long. If you are looking for a larger pub with both a lively and relatively boisterous crowd, John D. McGurk's in Historic Soulard is an Irish landmark known throughout the Midwest for its great Irish music, fantastic pub grub and drink, and its 8,000 square foot outdoor garden, complete with breathtaking landscaping, a waterfall, and two terrific outdoor bars. You can't go wrong with either of these places for future St. Patrick's Day celebrations.

Let's say live music and festive Irish environments don't tickle your fancy. Perhaps you are looking for a little bit of everything—an area that elicits a combination of classy, lively, clubby, and value-y. The Central West End appeals to a lot of students as a result of a varying mix of bars and restaurants that feature a predominantly younger crowd while continuing to maintain the relaxed, friendly atmosphere that St. Louis consistently exudes. If you are looking to get your grind on and impress members of the opposite sex by looking fly, hit up either Pepper Lounge or Mandarin Lounge on the weekends. Pepper offers two full bars and two dance floors as well as a VIP section with bottle service available for those who want to feel like high rollers...at least for one night. Mandarin employs a fusion theme with a rooftop deck that is perfect for spring and summer nights out with your friends or even random locals. Not the dancing type? Bar Louie is always a weekend classic with large portions of delicious bar cuisine and a vast selection of interesting beers, microbrews and wines by the glass or bottle. Don't miss out on $2.25 draughts on Thursday nights, or Friday and Saturdays that always generate a solid crowd and a generally good time for all those who attend. Cabs to the Central West End cost only about $10 from campus.

Although all of these areas present a wide variety of places to party, maybe you are looking for a new crowd to penetrate. If you want to take a break from the Wash. U. scene, try going to some of the SLU bars in Midtown to find some new friends or a new crop of members of the opposite sex. Head out to Humphrey's on Wednesday nights for penny pitchers (yes, literally 1 cent) starting at 11 p.m.. The Library Annex caters to the sports fans as well as the competitive drinkers with its fooseball, darts, billiards, shuffleboard, and of course, the best beer pong in St. Louis. Laclede Street Bar & Grill is another SLU favorite with

Going Out

great food and cheap drinks. The one bar that stands out to me the most in the SLU area is Harry's. Providing a spectacular view of downtown St. Louis from its sky deck, Harry's has a Friday college night special where guys drink for $15 all night and ladies drink for free from 10 p.m. to 2 am (though the drinks seem to taste strangely like water) with live music on the stage throughout the night. Just another perfect location for nights out in the spring and fall while the weather is still nice. Cab prices should hover around $15-20.

By this point, I hope you have a solid idea of how to branch out in St. Louis and have a good time. However, there is one more area of bars to introduce that will definitely give you a unique social experience in the city. The area is Historic Soulard just outside of downtown. Many of you may know it as the area through which the Mardi Gras parade runs. But what you may have not noticed is the abundance of bars surrounding the streets, some just hole-in-the-wall joints and others that seem like majestic outdoor drinking fests. Johnny's, Molly's, and the aforementioned J.D. McGurk's are just a few favorites. I could provide descriptions of over 30 bars and restaurants, but that's just too easy. Instead, I challenge you to explore them for yourself. Rally a group of friends together and make your journey through Soulard somewhat competitive or at least extremely exploratory. I'm talking about picking out between 5 -10 bars and creating your own Pub Crawl, or a personal favorite, Bar Golf. I am not saying you need to indulge in an excessive amount of drinking and stumble around in public; I am simply providing innovative ways to meander through one of the most unique and entertaining areas in St. Louis while grabbing one to several drinks as you casually mosey around with your friends and expand your St. Louis social horizons. You'll definitely meet some interesting characters on the way. And if you're lucky, you'll find a way to break the Wash. U. bubble and burst into the friendly and exhilarating social scene of St. Louis.

Top 10

10. Burning Kumquat, because everyone loves some post-coitus produce.

9. Any Sorority Suite in the Women's Building. Sorority sister optional.

8. Brookings Stage (bring some padding).

7. B-Stacks, Olin Library. Remember, inside voices.

6. Bathroom/Shower, 2nd Floor DUC. If you really feeling adventurous, do it between peak lunch rush hours, 12-2.

5. Butterfly Garden. No cocoons allowed.

4. Balcony of Graham Chapel = afternoon delight

3. Art Student Studios (Art Student Required)

2. Hammocks between Dardick and Nemerov/Village Quad. Moderate balance required

1. KWUR Studios. They will always have your love guru mix tape on the shelf.

Art of the One-Night Stand
Beating the curve in Orgasmic Chemistry

Attracting partners of the opposite sex at Wash. U. can be harder and more emotionally draining than finals week. With the self-imposed exclusivity of different social groups, be they library rats or B-School socialites, chances are you'll find yourself vying for a relatively small number of attractive bedmates. This in mind, chances are the drive for sexual satisfaction will have you pursuing some borderline cases you wouldn't normally talk to, and hopefully won't be talking to next week. But securing a one night stand can be a perilous journey, and sometimes even your stellar 3.78 GPA, New York heritage, Blackberry, and extensive student group involvement fall short in securing worthwhile partners. In this guide we'll examine a number of different strategies employed by Wash. U.'s most successful hookup artists.

The Library Whisperer
You've seen this guy hovering from one desk to the next on the third floor. Not only has he come just from the vending machine with some chocolate covered espresso beans to share, but he's got the "dopest study guide" he'd be willing to photocopy. He's focused, but not too focused, and wants to make sure that he's talked over all the material with you - just to make sure you both get it. It should be clear by this point, but make sure you know exactly what type of late night cramming he's talking about when the library closes and he invites you back to his dorm study room.

The Beer Pong Hero
Your team is down to its last cup, the opposing team sinks it. The beer pong hero rises to the occasion, and on the rebuttal hits all five of the opponents' cups in a row. Seven games and a lot of yelling and partial nudity later, the two of you are too probably too drunk to know which one of your rooms you've stumbled back to. Natty Lite might not be Aqua di Gio, but it'll work tonight, and unlike your shame you can wash away its tacky residue tomorrow morning.

Captain Catatonic
It's not until he's drained two thirds of the medicine-cabinet bottle of Segrams that Captain Catatonic really begins to work his game. There's probably something charming in his loveable dumb persistence, and

even if there isn't, rejection is a lot easier to handle when you can't seem to remember being rejected. Courage aside, it's not usually until two of these characters meet that either of them have any success. Here the normal pleasantries and flirtations give way to a more rudimentary animalistic form of dialog. Onlookers and passersby might not even be sure if the two are actually talking to each other, or just babbling to themselves. But if all goes according to plan, the two of them should stumble off in a matter of minutes. The one drawback Captain Catatonic runs is the possibility of not being able to remember whether or not they actually had a successful one night stand, thereby providing fertile grounds for their friends to make fun of them all of next week.

The Rando Classmate

Is that the quiet girl from your French class? You've never seen her out before, and she's wasted. Move in quick, banter a bit about your professor's unfair grading policies, and as luck should have it you'll end up in her dorm getting freaky. If you think it's weird now, just think about how weird it's going to be at 9:30 am next Tuesday/Thursday when you walk by her on your way to your desk. Just hope she doesn't tell her whole sorority about that thing you did with her goldfish.

The Gracious Host

Bedroom proximity aside, one of the benefits of a hosting a party is that you have the ability to lead private tours throughout your apartment to any of your guests. Have you got a balcony with a view of the arch? An elaborate spice collection? Want to go do some shots away from the crowd? Before trying this one out, make sure you've got a roommate or a close friend who can supervise the party while you're busy leading private tours of your, what was it, bedsheets?

Going Out

"Dating"

I have always asked myself what it means to date someone in college. Certain people can spend their entire college careers dating one person, only to break up a month after graduation. Others decide to go through college sleeping with anything that moves. How do you navigate the love landscape at Wash. U.?

We've already talked extensively about the attractiveness of the student body, but what does this mean for the dating scene? It means a) find a 10 and hold on to him/her as long as possible or b) learn to admire inner beauty instead of simply feigning it as a means of sexual conquest. Due to general ugliness, you will find average girls and guys who could barely find a date to prom swatting away potential suitors left and right. If this happens to you, don't let it go to your head. These people always suck.

What does the dating scene at Wash. U. look like? If one were to create a timeline in their head as to the process by which a relationship starts, one would presumably think that it all starts with asking a girl out for a cup of coffee, maybe a lunch, or perhaps a nice dinner and a movie. From there, if the young gentleman is lucky he will receive a kiss goodnight and hold himself back from calling the next morning. After a few more dates, the relationship may move to the bedroom and soon after: poof, a college couple is formed. The way it actually works in college is not quite the fairytale I have mentioned above. To be frank, a drunk guy and a drunk girl meet each other in the basement of some fraternity and go home together. This is repeated, ad infinitum, until phone numbers are exchanged and the two begin seeing each other on a more sober basis.

In college, relationships are usually the product of chance, as opposed to the deliberate hard work. They go out for some ass and in the morning realize they, to their surprise, might actually like the person they find lying there next to them.

I'm making this sound bad, and in some ways it is, however the college relationship truly is a beautiful thing. One of the best ways to stay happy at school is to have a significan't other to talk to and spend time with. You can have your girlfriends and your bros, but it's always nice to have someone else to come to at the end of the night. Who knows, you might even find Mr./Mrs. Right. Even if people haven't found that one and only special someone, people often think they have. Wash. U. students get in to very serious relationships that involve the most ridiculous of pet names, entire weekends watching movies, and public scoldings when one member acts outside of "established rules."

Now for all of you who want to get out there tonight and start holding hands with that special someone, I have a bit of advice. For guys, don't be surprised if a girl sees you coming off as too strong if you ask them out on a date. To ask a girl on a date in college means a lot more than it does in the real world, so if you choose to go down that path, make sure you know what you are doing. Don't get me wrong, some girls love that classic guy who will show up to the door with flowers and take them out to a nice Italian dinner. I'm just saying that in college, it's rare to hear of a relationship that will start that way. You may find better luck using a cheesy pick up line said with the confidence of a few Natty Lights.

I also want to make it clear that Wash. U. is not the type of place you are going to be able to set out on a night and bring someone back with ease. Girls tend to be on the pruder side, and guys tend to have less tact than Larry David at a funeral. If a girl doesn't go back with a guy it's most likely just as much his fault as it is hers, and if a guy is lucky enough to get a girl back to his room some kissing and spooning is about all he should expect the first night.

If you do find yourself in a relationship, Wash. U. really is a great place for it. Difficult work, an elusive social life, and a relatively small-sized student body are all factors that contribute to the reasons why having someone to talk to, sleep with, and get close to is an advantage here. Additionally, Wash. U.'s location makes it surprisingly romantic setting. Forest Park offers a plethora of activities, ranging from museum outings, to paddleboats, to hikes, and even great picnic spots. The Loop, Clayton, and the Central West End are all lively night scenes that flourish with restaurants, movie theaters, and even hookah bars.

There are exceptions to everything I have outlined here in this overview to dating at Wash. U., but I hope this gives you a sense of what the scene truly is like. Some people date one person for 4 years and others never find someone, nor do they ever want to. However both choices can lead to a very happy college experience with the opposite sex.

Going Out

Fake IDs

St. Louis, home of the Great American Lager, Budweiser. Residence of some of the best microbrews in the country. A drinkers paradise - as long as you are 21. If you want to truly enjoy all that St. Louis has to offer and aren't of age, you are probably going to need some type of fake ID.

Caution: There are serious consequences involved with having a fake, so follow this advice at your own risk. The following is for informational purposes only and is not intended to encourage or enable any illegal activity. We are not attempting to influence or persuade you to do anything illegal; we are simply describing a particular aspect of social life. The school has serious consequences if you are caught with a fake ID, so, once again, pursue one at your own risk...now that you've been warned, here's some information:

Real ID's
This is most common for those with siblings who are of age and girls. You borrow a real ID of someone and pretend that it is yours. The only risk you run is not looking enough like the person in the picture. Girls can get away with not looking anything like the person more often as bouncers are generally more privy to letting girls into bars. One common way that bouncers will try to weed out people using real ID's is to ask for a second form of ID. If you are using a siblings ID you may want to ask them for a credit card that has their name on it (you can even cancel it) so you have something else to show. Even if you don't have a family member who you can get an ID from, you can find someone who looks like you and is 21. If your a 5'7-5'9 male with curly brown hair, finding an ID shouldn't be too hard.

Good Knockoffs
These are the $200 fakes that your friend's friend's friend whose cousin works at a DMV can hook you up with. Usually California or Texas, these can "scan" and "black light." The defining quality of a good knockoff is having a good hologram. Even though these usually aren't even real holograms but gold dust that shines when light is placed on it, they tend to do the job. The thing to remember is that these are really hard to get

and that more often than not someone selling an ID is selling one of the type below.

Piece-Of-Crap Knockoffs

These are the Oregon, Maine, Florida, New Hampshire pieces of crap that rely on hope that the bouncer has no idea what the actual drivers license looks like. Generally these do not say driver's license and are not printed on actual PVC cards. These are going to work at bars where they take anything, but that's it. If a place is serious about not accepting bad ID's don't even try, faith will only get you a ticket.

But if all else fails, you got in to Wash. U., so you are probably smart enough to find a way to make your own - which is a felony.

Wash. U.phamisms:

30) B-Schooler- cl., Kid who is often wearing a suit, carrying a resume in a nice leather holder, bbming, planning on making a lot of money upon graduation, and born in Long Island.

31) Cluster-fucked- cl., This is when you have to register for a terrible schedule senior year just to fulfil clusters (this term will become extinct as the cluster system is phased out).

32) The Fun Room- p., It's not fun. That's really it.

Bars

Here's where you go to drink

Duffy's:

The historical go-to bar on Tuesday nights. Just a few minutes away from campus on Clayton Road, sitting behind Schnucks in a parking lot shared by UPS, Duffy's may not seem like an ideal place to throw a few back, but for a Tuesday it certainly does the trick. Known for its karaoke and cheap pitchers, those who are eager to start the week right will have a chance to get loose and have a great time.

The Good: Cheap beer that's close to campus.
The Bad: Drunk Wash. U. karaoke
The Ugly: Drunk St. Louisian karaoke

Three Kings:

Three Kings, formerly known as Riddles Penultimate, is located on the loop across from Chipotle and is known for having a huge variety of beers and live music every night.
The Good: Incredible food, incredible beer.
The Bad: Pricey, and the front room can get crowded.
The Ugly: The backroom. It's very lonely and remains unused unless the front is packed

Blueberry Hill:

The most famous bar on "The Loop" features a monthly concert by Rock n' Roll legend Chuck Berry. Though very tough on ID's, Blueberry Hill is one of the best bars in St. Louis. They've got a great dart room, the famous duck room where concerts are held, and a bar with a great selection of beer. Blue Hill also has great bar food, including their famous hickory burgers.

The Good: Chuck Berry, the dart room, the food
The Bad: The errant darts throw
The Ugly: The very errant darts throw

Moonrise/Eclipse:

After opening in 2009, the Moonrise hotel has emerged as a hot spot for Wash. U. students to grab a drink pretty much any day of the week. Its atmosphere is unparalleled--somewhat mimicking what would be a modern boutique hotel in New York City. The bar on the first floor, Eclipse, offers a fantastic selection of beers and high-quality food served late. The Moonrise bar on the roof of the hotel is incredibly comforting on warm evenings and offers views of the entire Delmar Loop. It's a bit classier than anything else you will find in the area, and serves mostly as filler for nights when not much is happening.

Good: A great martini is like sipping on a wet cloud- Woody Allen
Bad: Pricey drinks, and tough on IDs
Ugly: The view of your apartment being robbed while you watch from a distance

Oyster Bar:

Located off of I-64 on the 6th Street exit, Oyster Bar is frequented by upperclassmen in the early fall and late spring when the outdoor patio is prime for chilling. They are known for their oysters and alligator among other southern specialties. Yet most people enjoy Oyster Bar for its live music and vibrant atmosphere on the outdoor patio, which by the end of the night plays host to drunken dancing and out-of-tune singalongs. This is a great spot to go to with small to medium sized group of people, although it is common for the entire Wash. U. social scene to take over the bar, making the small space a bit claustrophobic.

The Good: Great service, bartenders make amazing shots, and awesome live music.
The Bad: When it rains, you're getting rained on.
The Ugly: The entire bar, but that's intentional.

Morgan Street:

Some people might call Morgan Street the cat's meow of college bars in

this town. Located on The Landing, "Mo Street" towers two floors, has three bars, a dance floor, billiards, and a patio for those warm nights. The beer is home brewed and sold cheap in pitchers, while drink and shot specials reign supreme. This is THE Thursday night spot, and its location next to a bevy of other great bars and casinos make it a great starting point for the night.

The Good: Great drinks to go along with the best scene of the week

The Bad: When three months into the school year, everyone gets bored of the bar, but continues to return out of habit.

The Ugly: Tough on ID's—a cop literally sits at the door.

Big Bang:

The bar after the bar, Big Bang typically plays host to the post-Morgan Street crowd. Located on the corner of Lacledes landing nearest Lumiere Casino, you will witness some of the most ridiculous drunken slurs to random 90's hits at this dueling-piano chain. It's also a wonderful place for that last minute hookup. Some love it, some hate it, but regardless almost everyone who is out on the landing ends up in here dancing and making out, committing post-freshman year floorcest with long-lost neighbors.

The Good: Amazing dueling pianists play your hits.

The Bad: Amazing dueling pianists play everyone else's hits.

The Ugly: When you wake up with a sticker on your jacket that says "Consider yourself banged" but no note on your nightstand (she broke my heart).

Market Pub House

The newest bar on the loop, Market Pub House has become a student favorite for going out on school nights. With karaoke on Tuesdays, $1 pitchers until 11 p.m. on Wednesdays, and Beer Pong on Thursdays, MPH is a great place to take a midweek break. MPH is also home to some cheap eats if your budget is tight. Burgers are only $1 on Monday's and wings are 40c on Wednesdays, which may say something about the food quality. While you can't expect a gourmet meal, you can expect to fill your stomach at the very least.

The Good: Cheap beer and food, and the warm nights out on the patio

The Bad: Usually empty before midnight

The Ugly: The toilet after one of those $1 burger

Bar Louie

"Hey _____ is having a birthday at Bar Louie tonight!" is usually the reason there will be a Wash. U. social scene at this restaurant with a bar. Although this Central West End establishment serves tasty American fair, it is simply not a bar fit for large college gatherings. If you're not going for $2 burgers on Tuesday, then you should only be going here because you got invited to a birthday party on Facebook that all your friends are going to. Even then, consider doing nothing.

The Good: Cheap burgers on Tuesday's
The Bad: The stains on your dress from drinks you spill on your way to the bar.
The Ugly: You're face after you reluctantly go to Bar Louie only to realize you're at a Bar Mitzvah.

Twisted Olive

The only thing that is smaller than the size of this Martini Bar is the number of people that know about it. Close to home on the Delmar loop, The Twisted Olive sits just above the hippie store, Sunshine Daydream. Given its miniature size, its a great spot to post up with a significan't other or a small group of friends for a few drinks. They have an extensive list of martinis that range from the classic to a Peach-Pomegranate martini, as well as some great beers and wines. When you walk into the Twisted Olive expect to have some conversation with the bartenders--the sight of people younger than 30 excites them. And if they don't feel like having conversation, it is probably because they are playing Playstation 1 on the projector screen. If you feel left out don't be afraid to ask for a chance to play, but don't be sad when they kick your ass in Crash Team Racing.

The Good: The Martinis and the Playstation
The Bad: The Once-A-Week DJ blasting music from massive speakers two feet behind your head
The Ugly: When the bartender is more drunk than you are.

Joey B's

If you're heading down to the landing early, and want to pregame for Morgan Street, look no further than Joey B's. A small bar with an eclectic clientele, Joey B's is the perfect place to get a few drinks, or shots, before moving elsewhere on the landing. The two things they are most famous for are their pizza (featured on Rachel Ray's Travels) and their shot menu, which consists of 124 different shots. These shots range from the classics such as 'the lemon drop,' to the very strong such as 'The Hell Breaker,' to the plain bizarre such as 'the who's your daddy.'

The Good: Shots! Shots! Shots!
The Bad: Shots... Shots... Shots...
The Ugly: When you're last in line for the bathroom.

Wash. U.phamisms:

33) T-Rex- cl., Now extinct quesadilla that contained, but was not limited too: cheese, chicken fingers, french fries, toasted ravioli, mozzarella sticks, marinara sauce, hot sauce. (Bon Appetit banned it a few years ago because it was irresponsible to serve students such a fattening meal, especially because no one actually remembers ordering the T-Rex. The only known evidence of a T-Rex is a dinosaur sized dump the next morning)
34) Pointersaurus Rex - cl., Do you dare try? The Pointersaurus Rex is the biggest pizza you will see--easily enough pie to serve 10 people. 28" inches in size, and 10 pounds in weight, this mamoth of a meal can only be transported with the help of two or more people. If you and a friend can finish a pointersaurus with two meat toppings in under an hour they'll gave you the pizza for free and hand you a check for $500.

205

Going Out

Conclusions...

So you reached the end of our guide, congratulations! You know everything there is to know about Washington University in St. Louis!

But not really. Wash. U. is an amazing place with so much to offer, and there is no way to stuff everything into a book, something that was never our goal. We hope that with this information you will be able to make better decisions when you get to school, so that you make the best of the short time you have. Of course you will make mistakes, but you have to learn from them. We certainly did. Wash. U. is your school. Make a difference! If there is something you don't like go ahead and change it. The students are the life of this university, and the administration understands this. Be the change you want to see.

Speaking of which, if you see something you think should be changed or added in subsequent versions of Bear It All, or you would like to get involved, please send an email to WUbearitall@gmail.com.

The End

Made in the USA
Lexington, KY
27 April 2014